CONNECTIONS

GENESIS-THE REVELATION-TODAY

DEBBI M HINTON

WESTBOW
PRESS®
A DIVISION OF THOMAS NELSON
& ZONDERVAN

WestBow Press books may be ordered through booksellers or by contacting:

WestBow Press
A Division of Thomas Nelson & Zondervan
1663 Liberty Drive
Bloomington, IN 47403
www.westbowpress.com
844-714-3454

Because of the dynamic nature of the Internet, any web addresses or links contained in this book may have changed since publication and may no longer be valid. The views expressed in this work are solely those of the author and do not necessarily reflect the views of the publisher, and the publisher hereby disclaims any responsibility for them.

Any people depicted in stock imagery provided by Getty Images are models, and such images are being used for illustrative purposes only.
Certain stock imagery © Getty Images.

Unless otherwise noted, scripture taken from the King James Version of the Bible.

Scripture quotations marked (TLB) are taken from The Living Bible copyright © 1971. Used by permission of Tyndale House Publishers, a Division of Tyndale House Ministries, Carol Stream, Illinois 60188. All rights reserved.

ISBN: 978-1-6642-2017-1 (sc)
ISBN: 978-1-6642-2016-4 (e)

Library of Congress Control Number: 2021901512

Print information available on the last page.

WestBow Press rev. date: 2/2/2021

CONNECTIONS is dedicated to Aunt Ruth Lunsford and LeAnn Arthur. Aunt Ruth is a godly lady, full of love and beauty and wit. We share so many lifelong connections including Faith in God, Gospel Music, Family, and a Passion for reading. In her 97 years, she has been an inspiration to everyone who knows her.

These connections have extended through the generations to my beautiful book-loving daughter, LeAnn Arthur. LeAnn has been my encouragement and computer expert during the preparation of this manuscript.

CONTENTS

INTRODUCTION
CONNECTIONS

GENESIS-THE REVELATION-TODAY

I am excited to begin this study of the Bible. It is NOT a deep study. I just want you to see that the BIBLE is very interesting, that it DOES APPLY to today. I hear so many folks say that the Bible is boring. Try this approach. I have read word by word the King James Version and chosen interesting and applicable portions for your review. Sometimes, I use The Living Bible. All quotes of scripture are from the King James Version unless listed as from The Living Bible.

God put a burden on my heart to STUDY the Word of God and to share it in a way that ALL could understand. Many people say that the Old Testament is boring and they cannot understand it. I need the Old Testament to help with understanding the New Testament and to be able to deal with the problems we currently experience in this world. I hope this writing has brought new light on the Old Testament and its importance in our personal relationship with God—our CONNECTION with God.

I have been blessed to LOVE numbers as you will see as you study this book. I am amazed at the number of people that Moses was ordained to lead out of Egypt. The correlation between the numbers which are frequently mentioned in the Bible intrigues me. But the most exciting number is ONE. One God. One Saviour. One lost soul that God counted worthy of the blood of Jesus. If there had been only you or only me, Jesus was willing to die for us. Grasp that concept.

It is important that we make the connections from Genesis and the creation (Yes, Jesus was a part of that) to the Covenant with Abraham, to the prophets, to the Birth of Jesus, to the beginning of the Christian Church until today and then to the Rapture. It is my desire that these connections will give us a better understanding of God and Eternity. I pray for EVERYONE who reads and studies this that our eyes will be opened to see the TRUTH and that we will one day meet in heaven.

Share your faith with others. This is the Great Commission at the end of the Gospels as Jesus was preparing for the Ascension.

Many years ago, I was blessed to attend a seminar with some godly people. The speaker looked at me during his presentation and said "to you who have been given much, much will be required". He knew nothing about me, but he sensed that God had blessed me abundantly. This is scriptural in Luke 12:48. I am so blessed that God has allowed me to live long enough to share this with you. May God bless you richly as you read and study God's word.

GET READY BE READY STAY READY

LESSON ONE
GENESIS

Genesis is FULL of wonderful lessons. Grab your BIBLE and let's dig. When you find a nugget, please make note and share with someone.

As Smith Wigglesworth, a British Evangelist born in 1859, said: "READ the WORD. CONSUME the WORD. BELIEVE the WORD. ACT ON the WORD." (The capitalization is added by this author, not by the evangelist.)

Second Timothy Chapter 2 Verse 15: "Study to show thyself approved unto God, a workman that needeth not to be ashamed, rightly dividing the word of truth."

Second Timothy Chapter 3 Verse 16: "All scripture is given by inspiration of God and is profitable for doctrine, for reproof, for correction, for instruction in righteousness."

Read Genesis 1:1–5.

List sources of light: _____

_____

What is light?

Genesis 1:2: Darkness on the face of the deep

Genesis 1:3: Did God create the light or Speak light into existence? What is the light of Genesis 1:3?

John 1:1–5: What is the light that shineth?

John 1:7: John was to bear witness of that light.

John 1:8: John the Baptist was not that light.

John 1:9: What is the true light?

John Chapter 1 Verse 10: "He was in the world, and the world was made by him, and the world knew Him not." Who is HE?

John Chapter 1 Verse 14: "And the Word was made flesh and dwelt among us, (and we beheld his glory, the glory as of the only begotten of the Father) full of grace and truth." WHO is the Word?

Genesis 1:14–19: What are the two great lights? Were these created before Genesis 1:3 or was God talking about a different light?

Genesis 1:6–13: Is the firmament what we call The Milky Way?

Read Genesis 1:20–31.

Note in Genesis 1:26, that humans were created in His image. God gave humans dominion over everything (in the sea, in the sky, on the earth).

How many times in Genesis Chapter 1 did God say that it was good? Genesis 1: Vss 10, 18, 21, 25. Very good in Genesis 1:31.

Genesis Chapter 2 is a recap of Chapter 1. Genesis 2:3: God rested. Genesis 2:7 tells us that God formed us from dust and then breathed life into us. This makes mankind different than any of the other animals. WE have a soul—a LIVING soul.

Chapters 3–11: Temptation: The beginning of sin. Genesis 4: 8: Jealousy led to murder. Genesis 4:9: God confronted Cain. Face/admit your sin. Genesis 4: 15: God put a mark on Cain. Genesis 5: 24: What happened to Enoch? Genesis 5:27: Methuselah was 969 years old.

Genesis 6:5: Evil and wickedness continually (sound familiar)?

Genesis 6: 8: What a testimony!

Genesis 6:14–16: Blueprint for the ark! 450 feet long x 150 feet wide x 45 feet tall. Three stories high. ONE window and ONE door.

Genesis 6:18: The covenant with Noah

Genesis 7:10: Seven days after Noah, his family, and the animals entered the ark, the rain started. Noah was 600 years old when the flood started!

Genesis 7:12: It rained forty days and forty nights.

Genesis 7:23: Everything outside the ark was destroyed.

Genesis 8:1: A wind

Genesis 8:2: Fountains of the deep—Springs in the ground?

Genesis 8:4: Seven months and seventeen days after the rain started, the ark came to rest on Mt Ararat.

Genesis 8:7: Noah sent out a raven. Did it return or continue to wander until the flood dried up?

Genesis 8:8: Noah sent a dove out three times. The second time it returned with an olive branch. The third time, the dove did not return.

Genesis 8:13: At the age of 601, Noah and family and the animals left the ark

Genesis 8:20: Noah built an altar to worship God

Genesis 9:13: A rainbow—God's promise. We still have rainbows today.

Genesis 9:21: Noah drank of the vine of his vineyard and got drunk.

Genesis 9:29: Noah lived 950 years.

Chapter 10: Nations grew.

Chapter 11: Tower of Babel.

Genesis 11:29: Abram married Sarai

Genesis 11:31: Terah took Abram and Sarai and Lot and was headed to Canaan, but he stopped to live in Haran.

Chapters 12–22: 12:1: Get out of town. Read Acts 7:2, 3.

12:2,3: Blessing from God. Read Acts 7:3.

12:5: Abram, Sarai and Lot entered Canaan.

12:10: Why did Abram move to Egypt?

12:12, 13: Abram told Sarai to tell everyone that she was his sister because she was beautiful.

12:18: Pharaoh was angry that Sarai and Abram had lied about her being the sister instead of the wife and he kicked them out of Egypt.

13:6: Abram and Lot became so wealthy that the land could not contain them.

13:11: Abram gave Lot the choice of lands and Lot chose Sodom. 13:12: Abram returned to Canaan.

13:14–17: God blessed Abram again.

14:11, 12: Lot and his family and his possessions were captured.

14:16: Lot was redeemed by Abram.

15:5: God blessed Abram again.

15: 13: God told Abram that his seed would dwell in a strange land and be afflicted there for 400 years. Follow this prophecy. It happened.

16: 16: Sarai was barren. She gave her servant (Hagar) to Abram. Hagar birthed Ishmael.

17: 5: Abram was renamed Abraham.

17:11: Circumcision? What is the importance of eight days old? There is medical evidence today about clotting factors at this age.

17:15: Sarai became Sarah.

17:16–21: Sarah to have a son at ninety while Abraham was 100.

In Chapter18, Abraham was visited by three angels. They reaffirmed that Sarah would have a son.

18:20–33: Sodom and Gomorrah were so wicked. God would not destroy the cities for fifty, forty five, forty, thirty, twenty or even ten godly men. Even ten godly men could not be found.

19:2–26: Angels visited Lot and helped him to escape. His wife became a pillar of salt when she turned to look back at the burning city.

19:31–38: The first reported Incest.

19:37: Moab was born. Was he the father of the Moabites?

20:2: Once again, Abraham told the people that Sarah was his sister. Remember Genesis chapter 12? How did that turn out for Abraham and Sarah?

21:1–6: Isaac was born. Abraham was 100 years old.

22:1, 2: God talked to Abraham and told him to offer Isaac as a burnt offering.

Genesis Chapter 22 Verses 7, 8: Isaac asked "where is the lamb?" Abraham said "the Lord will provide".

22:13: A ram had been caught in the thicket. Abraham sacrificed it instead.

22:14: Jehovah Jireh –The God Who Provides.

Chapter 23: Sarah died.

Chapter 24: Vss 1–13: Abraham told his oldest servant to put his hand under Abraham's thigh as a promise to Abraham that Isaac would not be allowed to marry a Canaanite woman. The servant was sent back to Abraham's home country to find a bride. How was he to know the right woman? Abraham and Nahor were brothers. Nahor's wife was Milcah. Milcah birthed Bethuel. Bethuel was the father of Rebecca and Laban. Vs 19: The first dowry?

Chapter 25: Vs 1: Abraham married again. Vs 6: Abraham had concubines. Abraham gave gifts to the sons of these concubines and sent them away. Vs 7, 8: Abraham died at 175. Vs 20: Isaac was a forty year old bridegroom. Vs 21: Rebecca was barren for twenty years. Isaac prayed. Rebecca conceived twins that struggled in the womb (Vs 23). God said these twins were two nations. Jacob was hanging on to Esau's heel during the birthing process. As the oldest son, Esau had the birthright but sold it to Jacob for food (Vs 29).

Chapter 26: Famine. Vs 2: God told Isaac not to go to Egypt at that time, but to remember the Covenant (Vss 4, 5). Vs 7: Isaac told the men of Gerar that Rebecca was his sister. (See Chapter 12.) Abraham had gone to Egypt during a famine and told the Egyptians that Sarai was his sister.

Chapter 27: Mother encouraged sibling rivalry. In chapter 25 we see that Jacob finagled the birthright. Rebecca helped Jacob to also steal the blessing that Isaac had intended for Esau. Vs 41: Esau vowed to kill Jacob after Isaac died. Vs 42: Rebecca told Jacob about Esau's vow.

Chapter 28: Vs 1: Isaac told Jacob not to marry a Cannanite woman. Sound familiar? See Chapter 24. Vs 2: To go to Mother's homeland in search of a wife. Vs 12: Jacob's ladder. God spoke to Jacob in a dream. Jacob named the place Bethel (this is the same place that God showed Abraham all the land that God would give him in Chapter 12).

Chapter 29: Vs 6: Rachel brought the sheep to water. Vs 10: Rachel was Laban's daughter. Laban was a brother to Rebecca. Jacob and Rachel were cousins. Vs 18: Jacob offered to serve Laban for seven years for Rachel who was beautiful. Her older sister, Leah, was tender eyed (had blue eyes which were a sign of weakness in those days). Vs 23: Laban tricked Jacob and gave him Leah instead. Vss 27, 28: One week later, Jacob married Rachel. Vss 32–35: Leah had Reuben, Simeon, Levi, Judah.

Chapter 30: Vss 1–8: Rachel gave her maid, Bilhah, to Jacob and they had two sons Dan and Naphtali. Vss 9–13: Leah gave her maid, Zilpah, to Jacob and they had two sons Gad and Asher. Vss 17–21: Leah had Issachar and Zebulun and a daughter Diana. Vss 22–24: Rachel had a baby and named him

Joseph. Read Vss 14 and 15: What is the significance of the mandrakes? Was this the first Viagra? Or did it increase fertility in the woman? Vss 25, 26: Jacob wanted to go home. Laban did not want him to go because he realized how much he had been blessed while Jacob was there working the herds. The rest of the chapter talks about an agreement that they had about the spotted/striped cattle. Interesting Veterinary science at work here with the green poplar, chestnut and hazel nut trees. Vss 42, 43: Jacob was blessed abundantly with strong cattle.

Chapter 31: Vs 3: God told Jacob to go home and that HE would take care of him. Vss 17, 18: Jacob, wives, children and flocks left for home. Vs 24: Laban was mad that Jacob had left and went after him. God told Laban to go easy on Jacob. Vss 28–41: Jacob had served Laban twenty years. Vs 49: Prayer of Mizpah. Jacob and Laban did not trust each other. They parted ways and each headed home.

Chapter 32: Jacob sent messengers ahead to locate Esau because he was afraid of Esau. The messengers returned to tell Jacob that Esau was coming with 400 men. Jacob was scared but remembered God's promise to protect them. He separated the people and the flocks and set up a gift for Esau of many cows, sheep, goats, camels and donkeys and sent those ahead with the messengers to Esau.

Chapter 33: Esau welcomed Jacob. God had kept his promise. Jacob delivered his gift to Esau. Jacob was disobedient and moved to Shechem (at Canaan) instead of returning to his homeland.

Chapter 34: Diana, daughter of Jacob and Leah decided to go out and see the world. God did not want his people to mix with the world. Trouble pursued. She was defiled by a foreign prince. The prince came to make a deal with Jacob to rectify the situation. Jacob's sons told the prince that all of the males in their country had to be circumcised. They agreed, because there would was much to gain by trading with Jacob. However, Simeon and Levi killed all the men while they were still sore from the circumcision. Then they spoiled the country and took all the animals and the women and children. Jacob was more worried about how he would be perceived than about the wrongs done by his sons.

Chapter 35: Vss 1–7: Some of Jacob's household worshipped strange gods. Jacob told them to get rid of them as well as their jewelry and to clean themselves up because God had told him to go back to Bethel (House of God). While there, Deborah, Rebekah's nurse died and was buried at Bethel. Vs 10: Jacob was renamed Israel. Vss 11, 12: Revisits the covenant. Vs 18: Rachel died giving birth to Benjamin. Vss 27, 29: Israel visited Isaac. Isaac died at 180 years old and was buried by Jacob and Esau.

Chapter 36: Esau was nicknamed Edom. Once again, we see that Jacob and Esau had so much wealth and cattle that the land could not support them (remember Abraham and Lot)?

Chapter 37: Jacob lived in Canaan. Joseph was seventeen at that time. Vs 3: Israel loved Joseph more than any of the other sons and gave him a coat of many colors. Vs 4: Jealousy. Vss 5–10: Joseph dreamed two dreams and told his father and brothers. Vs 14: Israel sent Joseph to check on his brothers.

Chapter 38: The story of Judah and his transgressions.

Chapter 39: Vs 4: Joseph became overseer in Pharaoh's house. Vss 7–19: Pharaoh's wife pursued Joseph. Vs 20: Joseph sent to prison. Vss 21–23: Joseph was established as a ruler over the prisoners.

Chapter 40: Pharaoh's butler and baker were thrown into jail. They had dreams which Joseph interpreted.

Chapter 41: Pharaoh dreamed but no one could interpret. The butler told Pharaoh about Joseph interpreting their dreams. Vss 15–24: Pharaoh told Joseph his dream. Vss 25–31: Joseph interpreted that there was a famine coming. Vss 32–36: Joseph told Pharaoh what to do. Vs 41: Pharaoh set Joseph over the land of Egypt. Vs 46: Joseph was thirty years old. Vss 50–52: Joseph and Asenath had two sons: Manasseh and Ephraim. Vs 57: Every country came to Egypt for food and corn.

Chapter 42: Israel sent the ten oldest brothers to Egypt to buy corn and food. Joseph knew them but they did not know him. Joseph accused them of being spies and put them in prison for three days. He told them that he would only believe that they weren't spies if they went home and brought back the baby brother. Simeon stayed in jail as security until the others returned. Joseph returned their money in their sacks with the grain. Israel refused to let Benjamin go to Egypt.

Chapter 43: Israel relented because the famine worsened and he sent Benjamin to Egypt with the other brothers along with gifts of spices, myrrh, nuts, and honey. Joseph had a feast prepared for the brothers. Vs 26: The brothers bowed to Joseph (See Chapter 36—Joseph's dream). Joseph had to go to his quarters to weep because he was so overcome at seeing Benjamin. He returned and they ate the feast.

Chapter 44: Joseph ordered that all the sacks be filled and that his silver cup be placed in Benjamin's sack along with the money that Benjamin had brought. Joseph sent his men to chase them down in pretense of looking for a stolen silver cup. Judah and the brothers returned to Joseph's house and fell on the ground before him (Don't ever say never). Judah offered himself in place of Benjamin.

Chapter 45: Joseph sent all of the Egyptians out of the room so that he could have a reveal reunion. He wept loudly and told them that he was Joseph. Vs 7: Joseph told them that what they had meant for evil had been worked for good by God. He had been placed in Egypt to have knowledge and wisdom during the fruitful years to save people during the famine. He sent them home to bring back Israel and the family. He promised them they would live in Goshen. He sent food, money, clothing and wagons for the trip.

Chapter 46: Vss 1–4: God spoke to Israel to go to Egypt. God promised safety. Sixty-six people came into Egypt. (Exodus 12: 37 and 40 tell us that 600,000 men plus women and children went out of Egypt 430 years later. Remember God's promise to Abraham in Genesis 15:13). Vs 34: Joseph's family moved into Goshen because shepherds were an abomination to the Egyptians. (And to whom did the angels appear when Jesus was born?)

Chapter 47: Vs 7: Israel blessed Pharaoh. Vs. 9: Israel was 130 years old. Vs 20: Joseph bought all of the land in Egypt (except the Priest's lands) for Pharaoh. The Egyptians sold willingly in order to have food. Vs 26: The people were to give 20% of everything to Pharaoh. VS 29: Israel told Joseph to put his hand under his thigh as a promise not to bury him in Egypt (Remember the hand under the thigh in Genesis 24: 1–4)?

Chapter 48: Israel blessed Joseph and his sons.

Chapter 49: Israel died.

Chapter 50: Vs 13: Israel was buried in Canaan. Vs 24: Joseph told his family that God would bring them out of Egypt and into the land God promised to Abraham, Isaac and Jacob. Vs 26: Joseph died at 110 years old, was embalmed and placed in a coffin in Egypt. Did they leave his body there?

Read Hebrews 11:22: The blessing of Abraham came to the gentiles. We can receive the Holy Spirit through faith.

The first prophecy of Christ is found in Genesis chapter 3
The Sabbath day began in Genesis 2:2, 3
What caused the fall of man? SIN
Where are the Children of Israel at the close of the book of Genesis? EGYPT

Four outstanding events in Genesis:
1. Creation
2. The Fall
3. The Flood
4. The tower of Babel

Four outstanding persons in Genesis:
1. Abraham
2. Isaac
3. Jacob
4. Joseph

LESSON TWO

EXODUS

Forty chapters. Written by Moses. Read Luke 24:44. Exodus means going out. Exodus is the book of REDEMPTION. Redemption through the power of God. Genesis 46:27 states that there were about seventy members of Jacob's family that came to Egypt. Exodus 12:37 says that there were about 600,000 men (plus women and children) that made the exodus out of Egypt 430 years after it was prophesied in Genesis 15:13 by God to Abram. This is confirmed in Galatians 3:16, 17.

Put on your imagination and picture the vastness of the exodus out of Egypt. In addition to all the men, women and children, there were herds and flocks. According to research, the population of Washington DC was about 712,000 in 2019. Moses led more than this for forty years of traveling. Moses had his hands full of whining, complaining people!

Chapter 2: Vss 8–10: The new ruler of Egypt did not know Joseph and he was afraid of the Israelites. The harder he worked the Israelite slaves, the stronger they became and the more they multiplied. NOTE: We grow stronger through adversity. Vs 16: The king of Egypt ordered all Israelite baby boys less than two years old to be killed. The next leader, Moses, was hidden by his mother in a little ark made of bulrushes. The daughter of the Pharaoh saw the baby and fell in love with him. She rescued him and hired his own mother to nurse him. We learn that for forty years, Moses lived in the palace of the same man that had ordered his death. Then Moses fled Egypt and went to Midian where he married and lived for forty more years. It was at Midian that God called Moses through the burning bush to FREE THE CHILDREN OF ISRAEL from Egypt.

Matthew 2: 16 tells us about Wise Men, King Herod, and baby boys under the age of two being killed. Both of these kings were afraid that an Israelite would take over their kingdom. The King of the Jews did not come to overtake a throne, but HE DID come to free the people – from SIN.

Moses was a shepherd in Midian. Jesus is known as the Good Shepherd. Moses raised lambs to be offered for blood sacrifice. Jesus IS THE LAMB - - THE ULTIMATE SACRIFICE.

Chapter 3: God sent Moses to Pharaoh. God foretold that Pharaoh would not release the Israelites easily because they were free labor. Then God foretold the plagues. Vs. 22 tells the Israelites to borrow from the Egyptians.

Chapter 4: Excuses. Moses had some. Moses was afraid. God started showing Moses some miracles. The rod became a snake then became a rod again. The water that Moses dipped out of the river turned to blood. Even with all this, Moses still had excuses. See verse 10. God gave Moses a mouthpiece—his own brother Aaron. Aaron was a prophet for Moses (one who speaks in the place of). Vss 19–21: God told Moses to go to Egypt, that Pharaoh would harden his heart and would not let the people go. Vs 27: God sent Aaron to find Moses. They gathered the elders together and taught them what God had instructed them.

Chapter 5: Moses and Aaron told Pharaoh that the Lord God of Israel said "let my people go" in Genesis Chapter 5 Verse 1. God called them His people! Pharaoh denied knowing God and refused to let them go. Pharaoh called his taskmasters and told them to make the Israelites gather the straw in addition to making the bricks. The Israelites were beaten when they could not meet their quota. Moses complained to God because the Israelites complained to him.

Chapter 6: Vs 4: God reminded Moses of the Covenant. He told Moses that He heard the groaning of the people. God told Moses to remind the people that "I am the Lord" in Exodus Chapter 6 Verse 6 and that He would deliver them. How many times did God remind Moses and the Israelites in Chapter 6 that he is the Lord? (Vss 2, 6, 7, 8, 29)? Did they not listen? Were they hardheaded? Were they non-believers? How many times and ways must He show us today that He is the Lord?

Chapter 7: Vs 2 tells us that Aaron was to speak to Pharaoh. Vss 9, 10: Aaron's rod became a serpent in front of Pharaoh. Vss 11, 12: Pharaoh's magicians threw down their rods also and their rods became serpents. But Aaron's rod-serpent ate the other rod-serpents. Throughout chapters 7–10, we see Aaron's rod used for many of the signs and wonders. Vss 17–25: The river turned to blood. In fact, all of the water turned to blood. The fish died. There was nothing to drink. For seven days there was nothing to drink. What a stink.

Read Psalm 105.

Chapter 8: In Egypt, snakes were worshipped, frogs were sacred. The Egyptians worshipped the Nile. Frogs croaked everywhere. Can you imagine the stench? Still Pharaoh would not let the people go. Vs 16: Aaron stretched out his rod and the dust of the land became lice. Once again Pharaoh would not let the people go. Vs 21: God promised there would be swarms of flies everywhere in Egypt except in Goshen where the Israelites lived. When God removed the flies, Pharaoh said no again.

Chapter 9: Vs 6: All of the cattle of the Egyptians died, but the cattle of the Israelites were spared. Pharaoh still refused to release the people. Vs 11: Painful boils appeared on all the Egyptians and their beasts. Pharaoh refused again. Vs 16: Who was God talking about? See Romans 9:17. God was using Pharaoh (surprise?) to show God's power and that God's name would be declared throughout the whole earth! God can use the most hardhearted person to show His power. Vs 23: God sent thunder and hail and fire that ran along the ground. Any person or beast that had been left in the open was smitten along with the crops in the field. None of this occurred in Goshen. Ever hear a testimony that was insincere? Read Vss 27, 28. Pharaoh admitted his sin. He made promises again. Vss 34, 35: Lying again.

Chapter 10: : Up to this point, God had been doing things to let Pharaoh know who HE is. Vss 1, 2 say that God told Moses and Aaron that He wants these things told to future generations so that they (we) will know their history and the greatness of God. Vs 12: Locusts with their beady eyes. We still have these today. Are these a reminder of the plagues that God can send? Vs 13 says the locusts came in on the East Wind. There were so many of them that it appeared to be darkness on the land. Vss 16, 17: Once again Pharaoh confessed and begged. Vs 19: The locusts were taken out of Egypt on a strong West Wind. Vss 22, 23 tell of the darkness over the land that was so dark that the Egyptians could not see each other for three days. However, the Israelites had light to see. Remember another time that an unusual darkness covered the land? See Matthew 27:45. This darkness covered the land for three hours when Jesus was on the cross.

Chapter 11: Borrow from your neighbors. The Israelites had found favor in the sight of the Egyptians and the Egyptians gladly gave them what they requested. Vss 4–6: God said that He would kill the firstborn of people and animals. Vs 7: God told the Israelites to separate themselves from the Egyptians.

Chapter 12: Vss 5, 6: God said to separate a lamb or goat without blemish and less than one year old from the herd and to keep it apart for four days. Vs 7: They were to apply the blood of this animal to the doorposts. Why not apply to the threshold? The blood of the sacrificial lamb (Jesus) is never to be trodden under our feet. VS 11: They were to eat with their sandals on and their staff in their hand. In other words, they were to be ready to leave in haste. This was the first Passover. Passover is still celebrated. Vs 29: At midnight, the Lord smote all of the firstborn of Egypt (from the firstborn of Pharaoh down through the firstborn of the Egyptian herds. Vs 30: A great cry was heard throughout Egypt. Pharaoh called for Moses and Aaron and told them to get everyone out immediately, to take their herds and their flocks and go. The Children of Israel left! 600,000 of them plus women and children. What an exodus! See Vs 31. Salvation through the blood of the lamb. Deliverance and salvation still only come through the blood of the lamb. There is NO other way. BE PREPARED. Vs 46 told the Children of Israel not to share their Passover. We cannot give salvation to anyone today. It must be an individual decision. Special Note: Vs 46 says not to break a bone of the lamb. See John 19:32, 33.

Chapter 13: The beginning of the journey to Canaan. God told Moses to teach the people and to instruct them to teach their future generations about the exodus from Egypt and how to observe the Feast of the Passover. Vss 17, 18: God did not take them the shorter route which would have taken about forty days, but took them through the wilderness by way of the Red Sea. Vs 19: Moses took the bones of Joseph with him. Vs 21: God led them with a pillar of cloud by day and a pillar of fire by night.

Chapter 14: Vs 8: Pharaoh hardened his heart again (didn't he learn anything during the Passover?) and chased the Israelites. Vs 10: The Israelites were afraid when they saw the armies of Pharaoh in pursuit. Once again, the Israelites complained. Vss 13, 14: Moses told them not to be afraid, that God would fight for them and they should hold their peace. VSS 21, 23: Moses stretched his hand over the sea and the water stood up on either side. They crossed on dry land. Vss 27, 28: Moses stretched his hand over the water again and the waters rolled back together and Egyptians were destroyed. Vs 31: The Israelites saw this miracle and feared God/believed God.

Chapter 15: Vss 1–19: Moses and the Children of Israel sang praises to God. Read their praise. Vss 20, 21 show that Miriam led the ladies in dance and a song of praise. Vs 23: Bitter water. Vs 24: Complaining again. Vs 25: God told Moses to throw a tree into the water. It became sweet again. Vs 26: God promised to be their healer.

Chapter 16: Vs 2: The entire congregation murmured against Moses and Aaron. Vs 10: The GLORY of GOD appeared in a cloud. Starting at Vs 13, we see that God sent quail each night and manna each morning to the people with instructions to gather it fresh every morning. (Relate this to Bread of Life—Refresh every day). The manna that was kept overnight became wormy. One night a week, they were to gather enough for two days for the Sabbath—they were to rest on the seventh day. Vs 35 tells us they ate manna for forty years!

Chapter 17: Once again the people whined because they were thirsty. Moses even whined. God told him in Vs 6 to strike the rock. Water came out of the rock for the people to drink. Vs 8: Amalek came and started war. Vss 9––13: Joshua and the army fought Amalek. Remember Joshua later became a great leader. As long as Moses held up his hands, the Israelites were winning. When Moses tired and couldn't hold up his arms, the Israelites lost. To the rescue: Aaron and Hur held up his arms, they were his support. When we tire, we can call on God to send someone to hold up our arms.

Chapter 18: Jethro, Moses's father in law, brought Zipporah and their two sons back to Moses. Jethro saw that Moses was wearing himself out by hearing the complaints and problems of the congregation all the time, so Jethro suggested that Moses choose able bodied men of good report to judge the smaller cases. Moses listened to his father in law.

Chapter 19: All the people agreed to listen to God in Vs 8. Moses told the people to bathe, wash their clothes and prepare for the GLORY of GOD on the third day. God appeared in a thick cloud. Vss 16–25 tell us about God appearing to the people. Moses was called to the top of the mountain.

Chapter 20: God gave Moses the Ten Commandments.

Chapters 21–23: Laws given to the judges about the responsibilities of Master and Servants, Property Rights, and Religious Laws.

Chapter 24: Moses went back up the mountain. A cloud covered the mountain –The GLORY of GOD covered the mountain for six days. On the seventh day, God called to Moses out of the cloud. Vs 18: Moses went back up the mountain for forty days and forty nights.

Chapters 25–27: God gave Moses the blueprint for the Tabernacle and everything in it. Everyone was to bring an offering. The offering was not to be forced, but given freely. God gave instructions for the Ark of the Covenant. The top of it is the mercy seat. Exodus 25:22: God said that HE would meet with the people in the tabernacle and talk to them from the mercy seat. Exodus 26: 31–33: The vail was to separate the Holy of Holies from the rest of the tabernacle. Read Matthew 27: 50–53: When Jesus died, the veil was torn apart from the top to the bottom. The Ark of the Covenant was to be carried by poles—no one was to touch it. It was to be in the Holy of Holies. Inside the Ark are the tablets of stone which GOD etched, a jar of manna, Aaron's rod. (Hebrews 9:4.) The tablets were etched by the Finger of God. Read Exodus 31:18.

Chapter 28: God told Moses how the priests were to dress.

Chapter 29: God gave Moses instructions for the cleansing of Aaron and his sons to be priests. Vs 46: Once again, God reminded them that He is the Lord.

Chapter 30: The tabernacle was to be sanctified (cleansed) yearly. Perfume was made into holy anointing oil.

Chapter 31: A gifted member of the tribe of Judah was appointed by God for the crafting of the special affects of the Tabernacle. Read Hebrews Chapter Nine.

Chapter 32: Moses was on Mt Sinai forty days. The people got restless and demanded a god. Aaron, the High Priest, told them to bring their gold earrings. He melted these and made a golden calf for the people to worship. (Watch out for false leaders.) The people partied, drank, feasted and had an orgy. Vss 7–9: Watch the interaction between God and Moses as to whom the children of Israel belonged. Yet in Vss 11–13, Moses pleaded for the people. Vss 15, 16 say that the tablets of stone were the work of God and graven on both sides of the tablets. Vs 19: Moses broke the tablets. Vs 20: Moses burnt the calf, ground it into powder, and dumped it in the water. The people had to drink that water. Vss 21–24: Aaron made excuses for his behavior as well as the behavior of the people.

Chapter 33: Vs 2: God sent an angel to Moses. Vs 11: Moses and God communicated as friends. Vs 17: God KNEW Moses by name.

Chapter 34: In Vs 1, God told Moses to hew two more stones and that He (GOD) would write again. Vs 5: God descended in a cloud. Vs 28: Moses was on Mt Sinai for forty days again. Vs 29: Moses shone.

Chapters 35–38: In minute detail the tabernacle was constructed exactly as God had instructed Moses on Mt Sinai. The furnishings of the tabernacle were built accordingly also, including the Ark of the Covenant and the altar.

Chapter 39: Vs 43: Moses inspected the work and construction and blessed it.

Chapter 40: Vss 34–38: A cloud covered the tent and the GLORY of GOD filled the tabernacle. When the cloud was taken up, the people journeyed. When it was stayed, they stayed.

RECAP of Exodus: The Exodus from Egypt, the Law given, the building of the Tabernacle.

The Book of Exodus teaches us how to follow God.

Who is our Passover? JESUS

LESSON THREE
LEVITICUS

Leviticus was written by Moses. The name comes from the Levites who were the priests. It was written to show the Israelites how to live in fellowship with God. The Israelites were to be a separated people, just as we are today. Leviticus teaches us about the offerings and sacrifices.

Chapter 1: The burnt offering. This is the offering of consecration. See Romans 12:1.

Chapter 2: The Meal (or meat) offerings - Service

Chapter 3: The Peace Offering – Communion with God

Chapter 4: The Sin offerings. One was for the sin of ignorance. One was for the willful or deliberate sins. These are called trespasses. There were instructions for the priests who needed to make a sacrifice, the elders, the rulers, the congregation when it sinned, as well as for the common people. When each of these sinned, they were to lay their hands on the head of the young bullock being sacrificed. Why? To transfer their sin onto the beast. Why do we lay hands on people today?

Chapters 5–12: Describe the many sins and what was needed for redemption.

Chapter 13: The World's first Quarantine. Is it a boil? Is it Leprosy? Is it contagious?

Chapter 14: Leprosy was incurable. It is like sin—it spreads. Both are deadly. Medical facts about Leprosy: It is a bacteria, spread by droplets. It damages nerves. It is carried by armadillos, red squirrels, and primates. It can lead to blindness and kidney failure.

Chapters 15–17: How to cleanse depending on exposures.

Chapter 18: How many times does God remind the people that He is Lord in this chapter? Vss 2, 4, 5, 6, 21, 30. Read and reread 18:22.

Leviticus Chapter 19 Verse 2: "Ye shall be holy: for I the Lord your God am holy"

Were the Israelites a little slow to learn? Vss 2, 3, 4, 10, 12, 16, 18, 25, 28, 31, 32, 34, 36, 37: What do these verses have in common? Vs 32: Honor the elderly.

Chapter 20: If they worshipped other gods, they would be put to death. Read Vs 13.

Chapters 21,22: The laws of the Levites.

Chapter 23: Describes the Feast of the Tabernacles (Booths).

Chapter 24: What is blasphemy? If you blasphemed, you were stoned.

Chapter 25: Plant and till for six years. People and the land were to rest during the seventh year. The fiftieth year was the year of Jubilee when all debts were cancelled and all slaves were freed. There would be bumper crops to make up for the resting years. Vs 35 tells them to help a brother in need.

Chapter 26: Read 26:13.

Chapter 27: The first of everything belongs to God.

Our redemption is through the blood of Jesus Christ, who is our High Priest.

LESSON FOUR
NUMBERS

Numbers was written by Moses. It is the 4th Book of the Law.

First Corinthians Chapter 10 tells us not to be ignorant of the wilderness journey and not to complain.

Numbers in Latin is Numeri, in Greek is Arithmai.

As the name of this Book implies, it is a book of numbers—taking the census!

Chapters 1–4: A count of the males of the Israelite camp that were twenty years of age and older who were able to go to war. The number of people on their way to Canaan may totally astound you. According to The Living Bible, in Numbers Chapter 20, Verses 20–46, here is the census:

House of:	Number
Reuben	46,500
Simeon	59,300
Gad	45,650
Judah	74,600
Issachar	54,400
Zebulon	57,400
Joseph – Ephraim	40,500
Joseph – Manasseh	32,200
Benjamin	35,400
Dan	62,700
Asher	41,500
Napthali	<u>53,400</u>
TOTAL:	603,500

Remember these are just the males twenty years old and older who were able to go to war. Add to this number the elderly, the women, the children and the males less than twenty years old. What a number! Each of these groups of people were camped in groups assigned by God, they were not just scattered around the camp. Quite an army. They lived together and they marched together in this same sequence. The tabernacle was located in the center of the camp with these families in designated areas around it. Notice that the house of Levi is not in this count. They were exempt from any war as they were responsible for the Tabernacle. Aaron and his sons were the priests and therefore exempt from this count also, but the House of Levi took care of the construction, maintenance, and disassembling of the tabernacle as well as transporting it when the Israelites were on the move. The Book of Numbers gave instructions of how to set up, decorate, and how disassemble the tabernacle in very minute detail.

There were 22,000 males one month of age and older in the House of Levi.

Chapter 5: Sent the lepers out of the camp, including anyone with open sores. Vss 11–35: What happened to an adulteress? If there were no witnesses to testify against her and no proof, but the husband was jealous or suspicious, she was brought to the priest with a suspicion offering. Her hair was unbound. The priest required her to swear that she was innocent, then made her drink of the bitter water. If she had truly committed adultery, the water would make her thigh rot and her body swell. If she were truly innocent, the water would not affect her and she would soon become pregnant.

Chapter 6: Men or Women could take the vow of a Nazarite to dedicate themselves to a special service of the Lord. They were not to touch strong drink or even eat any grapes (yes even no raisins). They were to vow to never cut their hair. They could not go near any dead body. Numbers Chapter 6, Verses 24–26: "The Lord bless thee and keep thee: The Lord make his face shine upon thee and be gracious unto thee: The Lord lift up his countenance upon thee and give thee peace." What a blessing.

Chapter 7: A list of various sacrifices

Chapter 8: Regulations for the ordination of the Levites. Note: Vss 23, 24 tell us that the Levites began to serve at the age of twenty five and had to retire at the age of fifty.

Chapter 9: The Israelites were guided by a cloud during the day and the appearance of fire by night. When the cloud stopped, the Israelites pitched their tents. They were led by God.

Chapter 10: The priests used trumpets to call assembly. The use of trumpets to call assembly or the guide the armies remained in existence for several thousand years.

Chapter 11: Complaining again. When we complain, remember Romans 8:28. Vs 4 mentions a mixed multitude. Who were these folks? Were they sightseers? Were they folks within the camp who were not Israelites? Vss 10–15: Moses complained about the burden of leadership. He was at the end of his rope. Can you imagine traveling with so many people who complained and complained?

Look back at Exodus 19:17–26. Moses listened to his father in law and picked God-fearing men to be judges over the less complicated issues. Vs 16 tells us that God directed Moses to gather seventy men to be elders/officers. In Vs 17 God anointed the seventy. Vs 21: Moses and the people once again doubted God's provisions. Vs 22: Did you realize that in addition to all of the people, there were herds and flocks in this caravan? Vs 31: God sent quail to eat. Vs 33: A plague killed a large number of the Israelites.

Chapter 12: Miriam and Aaron talked against Moses because he had married an Ethiopian. Were they jealous? Miriam was afflicted with leprosy and was shut out of the camp for seven days.

Chapter 13: One man from each tribe was sent over into Canaan to spy out the land and the people. They spied for forty days. Only two of these men voted to go over into Canaan. The others thought the land and the people were too dangerous. However, Joshua and Caleb had great faith and encouraged the Israelites to go over into Canaan.

Chapter 14: Everyone murmured and complained against Moses and Aaron. God had brought them to the Promised Land. They just had to have the faith to enter and possess it. Fear robbed them of what God had promised over and over. These people even begged and plotted to return to the slavery of Egypt. After all they had seen and experienced, they let Satan defeat them with unbelief. THOUGHT: Are we any different today? Vs 21 tells us that all the earth would be filled with the GLORY of the Lord. In Vs 29 we learn that everyone twenty years of age and older with the exception of Joshua and Caleb would die in the wilderness and the young would wander in the wilderness for forty years. Think of the blessings these folks missed through unbelief. Forty years of wandering in the wilderness. Sometimes we are so close to claiming the promises of God, but we fail due to unbelief and complaining. Some of the people defied God and decided to go up the mountain to look over into Canaan. The Amalekites and the Canaanites came out and killed them.

Chapter 15: God taught Moses how to make sacrifices.

Chapter 16: Reuben's descendants rose up against Moses saying that Moses thought too highly of himself. In Vs 23 God told Moses what to do. In Vs 26 Moses told the other people to get away from this tribe and in Vss 31–33 we see that the earth opened up and swallowed them. Vs 41: Everyone complained again.

Chapter 17: Each tribe was to bring a rod to the tabernacle with their name inscribed on the rod. Aaron's name was inscribed on the rod of the House of Levi. Aaron's rod bloomed, blossomed, bore almonds. Aaron's family was chosen for the priesthood.

Chapter 18: One-tenth of the firstlings and first fruits of the harvest were to be for the temple. One-tenth of that went to pay the preacher (Aaron and his family). Remember that Aaron and his family did not own land and did not farm as they were the priests. If we depended on one-tenth of the tithe that people give today, would the preacher (priest) have enough to support his family? The remainder of the offerings went to the Levites for the care of the temple.

Chapter 19: The red heifer, without spot or blemish and had never been worked in a yoke, was to be sacrificed and the ashes used for the cleansing ritual. Today, we are still looking for the perfect red heifer. We will discuss this more a little later. You may wish to research this.

Chapter 20: Miriam died. Vs 2 tells us that there was no water again. Once again, the people moaned and groaned. Vs 6 says that Moses and Aaron went to the door of the tabernacle and fell on their faces before God. THE GLORY OF THE LORD appeared to them. Vs 8: God told Moses to go to the rock and to speak to the rock. Moses disobeyed and smote the rock two times. Water came gushing out. Vs 12: God told Moses and Aaron that they would never see the Promised Land because of this sin. Vs 14: Who is Edom? Genesis 36:1 says Esau became Edom when he married a Canaanite woman. Vss 14–21: Kadesh, the king of Edom, refused to let the Israelites pass through. Aaron died. His son Eleazer inherited the priestly robe.

Chapter 21: The people complained again. God sent fiery serpents that bit the people. God told Moses to fashion a fiery serpent out of brass and to set it on a pole. Anyone bitten by the serpents could just take a look at the brass serpent and be healed. Read John 3:14, 15. The king of the Amorites would not let them pass through the land. He made war with the Israelites and was killed by the Israelites. The Israelites possessed the land after that.

Chapter 22: Who are the Moabites? Remember Genesis 19:36 and 37. Lot's son by his oldest daughter was Moab. Balak was king of Moab and he feared the Israelites. He sent for Balaam (Balaam put curses on people). God told Balaam not to go. Balak sent for Balaam again. God allowed him to go but put an angel with a fiery sword in his way. Read the story in Vss 22–35.

Chapter 24: Balak was angry that Balaam would not put a curse on the Israelites. He sent Balaam home.

Chapter 25: Vs 1 tells us that the Israelites committed whoredom with the Moabites and worshiped the Moabite gods. Vs 9 tells us that 24,000 Israelites died because of sin.

Chapter 26: The Israelites were numbered again. 601,000 men over the age of twenty plus 23,000 males of the house of Levi.

Chapter 27: God chose Joshua to lead the people. Vss 1–11: Was this the first Women's Rights Movement?

Chapter 28: Instructions on various offerings.

Chapter 29: More about offerings.

Chapter 30: Vows are voluntary. Don't make them if you do not intend to keep them.

Chapter 31: Prepare for War. 12,000 Israelites killed the males of the Midianites. They took the women and children captive. They took the flocks and the goods of the Midianites and burned the cities. Vss 15–17 tells us that the Midianites lived in deep sin and had no morals. They offered human sacrifices—even their own children. Read this chapter to see the wealth that was captured. Vs 49 tells us that all of the Israelite warriors returned. Who were these Midianites? Remember when Abraham remarried after Sarah's death (Genesis 25:1, 2)? In Exodus 18:1, we learn that Jethro, the father in law of Moses, was the priest of the Midianites.

Chapter 32: The tribes of Gad and Reuben settled in Jordan outside of Canaan.

Chapter 33: Who wrote the going out (Exodus) of Egypt (Vs 2)? How many camping stops did the Israelites make after leaving Egypt (Vss 5–49)?

Chapter 34: The borders of Canaan and where each tribe was to settle.

Chapter 35: There were three cities of refuge in Canaan and three outside of Canaan. These were where people could go if they killed another person accidentally. They were only safe while inside these refuge cities.

Chapter 36: If a female inherited land, she had to marry a man of that tribe or she lost her inheritance.

LESSON FIVE
DEUTERONOMY

Deuteronomy is the 5th Book of the Law—written by Moses. Deuteros means 2nd. Nomos means law.

A study of the final preparations for entry into Canaan. This book is a review of the law to the second (the new) generation.

Chapter 1: Vss 8, 21: Moses addressed the Israelites in the fortieth year in the wilderness to go in and possess! Remember that this generation was less than twenty years old (or not even born yet) when the Israelites left Egypt. Vss 26–28: This new generation doubted God. Vs 30: God went before them. God fought for them.

Chapter 2: Vs 4: Passing through Esau's country (Edom). The people were instructed to pay the Edomites for water and food, but not to meddle with them. God reminded them that they had lacked for nothing in the forty years wandering in the wilderness. Vs 19: Don't meddle with the people of Ammon either.

Chapter 3: Dealing with giants. Vs 11 tells us that Og, the king, was a giant. His bed was made of iron and was thirteen and one-half feet long and six feet wide. A king-sized Bed. Vs 22: God reminded the Israelites not to fear for He would fight for them.

Chapter 4: Vs 1: Again, God told the people that they should go in and possess. Moses reminded them of some of the battles and commanded them to follow the Ten Commandments and to remember the Covenant.

Chapter 5: The Ten Commandments.

Chapter 6: Vss 4, 5 remind us of the Great Commandment. Read Matthew 22:35–39. Vs 6: The Israelites were to teach these laws as they made them a part of every minute of their lives.

Chapter 7: Vs 2 told them to not get involved with the idol worshippers, to make no covenants, to have no weddings with them. Vs 5: Break down the altars, destroy the idols. Vss 6–8: Read about God's love and redemption.

Chapter 8: Vs 2: Why did God lead them in the wilderness for forty years? (To humble them and to prove HIM). Their clothes did not wear out and their shoes fit all those years. Vs 10: Eat. Be full. Bless the Lord. We, like the Israelites, must learn to rely on GOD and then to PRAISE HIM.

Chapter 9: Vs 17: Moses literally broke the Ten Commandments. Moses reviewed the many disappointing times and how he had prayed to God to intervene.

Chapter 10: Vss 1–4: The second writing of the Ten Commandments. By whom? (Vs 2)? Per Deuteronomy Chapter 10 verse 12: "And now, Israel, what doth the Lord thy God require of thee, but to fear the Lord thy God, to walk in all his ways and to love him, and to serve the Lord thy God with all thy heart and with all thy soul." These WERE and ARE God's requirements.

Chapter 11: Vs 8: Be strong. Vs 11: It is a land of hills and valleys. Vs 14: First rain and the latter rain. It was their choice (and is still our choice). Vss 26–28: A blessing and a curse—a blessing for obedience and a curse for disobedience.

Chapter 12: Why did God tell them to destroy the altars and the pillars and to burn their groves? (To get rid of all of this and to get it out of their sight). Vs 31 tells us that the former Canaanites offered their own children as burnt sacrifices to strange gods.

Chapter 13: Don't get caught up in spiritualism or witchcraft. Fear God, shun evil, don't be tempted.

Chapter 14: Don't cut yourself. Vs 2 says to be holy, to be peculiar. Vss 3–21: Foods allowed and foods to absolutely not touch.

Chapter 15: Debts were to be cancelled every seven years. The debts of foreigners were not included in these cancellations. Even in those days, there were poor people among them. If they had slaves, the slaves were to be freed at the end of six years and they were to be given gifts. If the slave did not want to be free, he would have his ear pierced with an awl into the door.

Chapter 16: Instructions for keeping the Passover. Seven weeks and one day after the Passover is Pentecost. Read Acts Chapter 2 about the Day of Pentecost. Vss 11, 14 told them to rejoice. Vs 17 told every man to give freely.

Chapter 17: Anyone who worshipped other gods in front of two or three witnesses was to be stoned. Difficult matters were to be taken to the priests. Vss 14–20: Instructions for a king.

Chapter 18: The Levites had no inheritance. Vss 1–8 gave instructions for taking care of the Levites. Vss 9–12: Witchcraft allowed. Vss 15–22: Moses foretold about a prophet.

Chapter 19: Setting up cities of refuge. Why were they necessary? Who could use them?

Chapter 20: The Israelites were told to not be afraid in battle. Why? God was going before them to fight for them and to save them. If the people offered to make peace instead of war, that was honored but those people became servants of the Israelites. If they were not peaceable, they were to make war, to kill all of the males and to take the women and children and goods. There were to be no peace treaties.

Chapter 21: If no one knew who had killed a person, a heifer was to be beheaded, the elders were to wash their hands over the heifer. Vss 11–14: If a man saw a beautiful woman, he was allowed to take her home, shave her head and cut her nails and wait one month. Then she could become his wife.

Chapter 22: Laws of helping to take care of people's property. Vs 6: Cross-dressing was (and is) an abomination. Interesting notes: Put a railing around the roof of your house so no one falls to their death. Don't plow with an ox and an ass together. Adultery meant death to both participants.

Chapter 23: A eunuch was not allowed in the congregation. Acts Chapter 8 tells about the salvation of a Eunuch. This chapter in Deuteronomy lists people who are not allowed in the congregation.

Chapter 24: If a man didn't like his wife, he could divorce her. If she remarried and the second husband divorced her or died, the first husband was not allowed to take her back. Vs 5 tells how to stay out of the draft. **God's** welfare program - Gleaning.

Chapter 25: The story of the man who had his sandal pulled off. Instructions to use accurate scales.

Chapter 26: Bring the first fruits. Every third year there was to be a special tithe that went to the Levites, the widows and orphans and to migrants. Worship God wholeheartedly and be holy.

Chapter 27: How to build altars. How to make burnt offerings and peace offerings. A list of curses.

Chapter 28: Vs 2: Blessings would overtake them. Read Vss 1–14 about a long list of blessings. Then read Vss 15–46 for a long list of curses. Why the curses (Vss 45–47)? Because they weren't joyful and didn't listen to God. Read Second Kings 6: 26–30.

Chapter 29: The people had seen many things, but understood very little. They had food without planting.

Chapter 30: KEY VERSE!! Vs 19: Life and death. Blessing and curses. We each must choose. Choose life.

Chapter 31: Vss 15: Moses told the Israelites that he couldn't go with them into Canaan but that God would go with them. Vss 6, 7: Be strong and of good courage. Vs 10: They were instructed to read the whole law to everyone every seven years. Vs 14: God called Moses and Joshua to the tabernacle for Joshua's commissioning service. Vs 26: The Book of the Law was placed in the Ark of the Covenant.

Chapter 32: The song. When the song ended, Moses went up on Mt Nebo to look over into Canaan. He died there.

Deut 33: The blessings of Moses.

Chapter 34: Moses died. Vs 10 says that there was no other person like Moses. The Lord knew him face to face. Read Jude Vs 9. Michael the archangel disputed with Satan for Moses's body.

READ HEBREWS 11:23–29.

LESSON SIX

JOSHUA

Joshua means JEHOVAH is SALVATION.

The first five books of the Bible are from the beginning of time up to preparation to enter the Promised Land. Joshua led the Israelites into the Promised Land.

Chapter 1: Vs 2: God told Joshua to arise and cross over Jordan. Vs 5: God told him that no one could stand against him. Vs 6, 7, 9, 18 : Told them to be very courageous.

Chapter 2: Joshua sent two spies to check out Jericho. The spies lodged at Rahab's (a harlot) house. She hid them on the roof and covered them with flax because she knew they were of God. She asked them to save her family as repayment. She let them down through a window by a rope. She lived at the wall. She told them to go to the mountain. The spies asked her to put a scarlet thread in her window and to get her family inside the house. The spies told Joshua that the people were afraid of the Israelites.

Chapter 3: Vs 4: The Israelites were instructed to keep 3000 feet between them and the Ark of the Covenant. Count it. This is more than one-half mile between them. Vs 13: STEP into the water. The water separated.

Chapter 4: One man from each tribe was to take a stone from the Jordan and use those to build a monument so their children would know of the miracle crossing. Then Joshua built a monument in the middle of the Jordan with stones. The tribes of Reuben, Gad and the one-half tribe of Manasseh decided to live outside Canaan, they led the other tribes to Jericho just as Moses instructed.

Chapter 5: When the Amorites and the Canaanites heard about the crossing of the Jordan, they lost courage. There was a second round of circumcisions. This round was to those males born during the trip. Vss 11,12: The Israelites ate of the fruit of the land. No more boring manna. Vss 13-15: Who is the man with his sword drawn? Standing on Holy Ground.

Chapter 6: We all know about the battle of Jericho. For six days they made one trip around each day. On the seventh day, they made seven trips around. Where was the Ark of the Covenant during these days? Vs 4 says it was part of the marches. On the seventh trip on the seventh day, the seven priests blew the trumpets loudly, the people shouted and the wall fell flat. (The first twelve trips were made in silence.) Remember Rahab the harlot from Chapter 2? All of her family inside her house were safe. Vs 18: They were told not to take anything for themselves. Vs 19: The gold, silver, brass and iron were taken for the Lord's treasury. The Israelites went in and destroyed everything. Vs 23: Rahab and her family were brought out before the city was burnt. Vs 25 tells us that her family was saved for protecting the spies.

Chapter 7: Against God's orders, Achan took some things. This caused the Israelites to lose the battle at Ai. Achan and his family were stoned to cleanse the people.

Chapter 8: The Israelites split into two groups. One group went to declare battle while the other group hid in ambush. When the men of Ai came out to fight, the Israelites ran. The men of Ai chased them. The men who were hidden in ambush went in and set the city on fire while the soldiers were gone.

Chapter 9: A trick. The enemy came in acting like they wanted to be servants of the Israelites. Looks were deceiving. Joshua did not pray and seek God's guidance and fell into the trap of the enemy.

Chapter 10: Vs 11: See how God fought their battle. Vs 13: Talk about a long day. Why? Vs 12: Joshua asked God to have the sun and moon stand still. This describes how Joshua captured many cities with God in control. Vss 14 & 42: The Lord God of Israel fought for Israel.

Chapter 11: Key Verses: 15 & 23. Read them. God told Moses, Moses told Joshua. Much of Canaan (but not all) became the land of the Israelites. They finally rested from war.

Chapter 12: A listing of the countries captured and possessed by the Israelites. Remember that the tribes of Reuben, Gad and the one-half tribe of Manasseh settled outside Canaan. The area where Reuben's tribe settled is now called Jordan. Gad's tribe and the one-half tribe of Manasseh settled the area now known as the Golan Heights.

Chapter 13: Wait. Did the Israelites rest from war too soon? Joshua was getting old and there were still lands to conquer. Vs 22: Remember Balaam being talked to by his ass? He was killed by the Israelites.

Chapter14: Caleb was forty when Moses sent him into Canaan as a spy. Vs 10 tells us he was eighty five and still followed God and was still strong.

Chapter 15: Land assignments made. Vs 63: The Jebusites were allowed to remain.

Chapter 16: The Canaanites of Gezer were allowed to remain.

Chapter 17: More land assignments.

Chapter 18: The Tabernacle was finally set up. More land assignments. The first surveyors.

Chapter 19: Land assignments completed.

Chapter 20: Cities of Refuge

Chapter 21: Land trades arranged

Chapter22: Joshua reminded the Reubenites, the Gaddites and the one-half tribe of Manasseh of the Great Commandment in Vs 5. Vs 6: Joshua blessed them. There was a threat of war between those inside Canaan with those outside Canaan. Subject: An altar?

Chapter 23: Joshua began his farewell speech.

Chapter 24: More of the farewell speech. Joshua reviewed the exodus and the travels to the Promised Land. Joshua Chapter 24:15: "choose you this day whom ye will serve". Vs 28: Joshua died at 110. Did you notice as much whining and complaining under the rule of Joshua? Vs 31 tells us that Israel served God all the days of Joshua. Remember that Joseph did not want to be left in Egypt? Vss 32, 33 tell us that Joseph's bones were buried in the Promised Land!

LESSON SEVEN

JUDGES

Judges is a book of History. Who wrote it? Samuel.

Chapter 1: Judah and Simeon fought the Canaanites after Joshua's death. Vs 6: They cut off the king's big toe and thumbs. Vs 8. They burned Jerusalem.

Chapter 2: After Joshua died, the Israelites worshipped other gods.

Chapter 3: Vss 5–7: They lived among the Canaanites, Hittites, Amorites, Perizzites, Havites, Jebusites and they intermarried with them. They served the gods of these people. They did evil in the sight of God. They forgot God and served Baalim. There were wars.

Chapter 4: We meet Deborah and Barak. Read Vss 8, 9. Deborah and Barak marched to war against Sisero. Vs 15 tells us that Sisero ran away and went to the tent of Jael. She covered him with a blanket and drove a peg through his temple.

Chapter 5: Read Chapter 5. This is the song of Deborah and Barak. I prefer The Living Bible for this chapter as it is quite poetic. There were forty years of peace after this.

Chapter 6: The Midianites prevailed against the Israelites. Gideon was met by an angel. The Lord appointed Gideon to save the Israelites. In Vs 16 God told them that he would be with them. Gideon did not believe it so he put out a fleece twice. Vss 37–40: Have you ever put out a fleece? Is it a good idea?

Chapter 7: Jerubbael was also known as Gideon. Gideon's army was too big. He had 32,000 against the 135,000 but God was trying to prove that HE would fight their battles. Time to thin the troops. 22,000 left because they were afraid. God said that there were still too many. How do you drink from a stream? 300 cupped their hands and lapped the water. These 300 were chosen to go to war.

Gideon snuck into the Midianite camp at night and heard a man tell about his dream. The dream meant that the Midianites were afraid of the Israelites. He went back to the camp and woke up the 300 men. He divided the 300 men into three groups. Each man was given a trumpet and a clay jar with a torch. They surrounded the Midianite camp. Upon the signal, they blew their trumpets, broke the clay jars with the torches inside and held the torches high. Judges Chapter 7, Verse 20 of The Living Bible tells us that they yelled "For the Lord and for Gideon". The Living Bible tells us in Judges Chapter 7, Verse 22 tells us that the Midianites panicked and started killing each other.

Chapter 8: The fall of Gideon.

Chapter 9: Abimelech (one of Gideon's seventy sons) became King. There was bad blood against Abimelech. Vs 53 tells us that a woman killed him.

Chapter 10: More leaders came and went. Vs 6 tells us that Israel did evil in the sight of God. There was more fighting.

Chapter 11: Jephthah was the son of a harlot. His half brother kicked him out of the family. When threats came, they wanted him back and he was made a captain. His daughter was offered as a burnt offering to fulfill a vow he made.

Chapter 12: Jephthah ruled for six years. There were rulers and more rulers over the next several hundred years.

Chapter 13: Vss 2, 3: The wife of Manoah was visited by an angel who told her that she would have a son. She had Samson. Samson was a Nazarite—he was to never cut his hair.

Chapter 14: Vss 5, 6 tell how Samson killed a lion with his bare hands. Later, there was honey growing in the lion's carcass. He ate the honey. Judges Chapter 14 Verse 14 says "out of the eater came forth meat, and out of the strong came forth sweetness". This was Samson's riddle. Samson wanted to marry a Philistine woman. He made a feast and there were thirty men at the feast. He promised them a change of clothes and some sheets if they could answer his riddle. The men could not solve the riddle so they threatened Samson's wife to learn the answer. She used her female charms to entice the answer from Samson. When the men answered the riddle, Samson became angry. Read Vs 18. The woman ended up marrying another man.

Chapter 15: Later, Samson tried to return to get her. He tied 300 foxes together by their tails two by two with a lighted torch between them and sent them through the fields to burn the corn, the olives and the vineyards of the Philistines. The Philistines retaliated by burning his former wife and her father. Samson went to live in a cave. 3000 men of Judah went to get him to deliver him to the Philistines. He broke the ropes that bound him and killed 1000 of the men with the jawbone of an ass. Then he was thirsty and God gave him water.

Chapter 16: Samson, the man who was so strong physically, was so weak with females. He went to a harlot. He loved Delilah. The Philistines told her to learn the source of his great strength. He taunted her and lied to her about it. She got mad and pouted. Vs 17 reveals his secret. She had his hair cut and his eyes blinded. He was captured by the Philistines. Vss 29, 30 tell us he destroyed the house and everyone in it including himself by collapsing the pillars of the house. Vs 31 tells us that Samson was a judge over Israelites for twenty years.

Chapter 17: Yet another story of the degeneracy of the Israelites.

Chapter 18: The tribe of Dan looked for a place to call home. They stole Micah's idols and his personal priest. Micah was a Levite. Micah chased them but quit when he realized they were too strong. The Danites attacked the country of Laish, killed the people and occupied that land.

Chapter 19: Read Judges 19. Does this sound familiar? Read Genesis 19. How did that story end? What is the significance of the twelve pieces?

Chapter 20: There was bitter fighting against the tribe of Benjamin.

Chapter 21: The men of the tribe of Benjamin went looking for wives because the men of Mizpah had said that they would not let any of their daughters marry into the tribe of Benjamin.

NOTE: The book of Judges tells of great failures because the Israelites worshipped false gods and neglected God. Just as the sinfulness of man is constant, SO IS THE MERCY OF GOD!

LESSON EIGHT

RUTH

A great love story. Ruth was a Moabite—a descendant of Lot.

Chapter 1: Elimelech and Naomi took their sons, Mahlon and Chilion, to Moab because there was a famine in Judah. Elimilech died in Moab. Mahlon and Chilion married Moabite women. Mahlon and Chilion both died. Naomi heard that the famine had lifted in Judah and made plans to return home alone. She told her daughter- in-laws to remain in Moab and to remarry as they were young and had no children. The second time she told them to stay, Orpah decided to remain in Moab but Ruth insisted on going with Naomi, so Naomi and Ruth went to Bethlehem of Judah.

Chapter 2: Ruth went to glean corn. Remember God's welfare plan? (People worked for it. They did not sit around and wait for handouts.) Read Leviticus 19:10 and 23:22. Ruth ended up in the fields of Boaz. Boaz was kin to Elimilech. Boaz told Ruth to ONLY glean in his fields and then told his harvesters to leave her alone and to leave extra in the fields for her to glean.

Chapter 3: When Ruth returned home, Naomi was excited that Ruth had gleaned so much and that she was working in the fields of Boaz, a kinsman. She told Ruth to go to the threshing floor that night and watch where Boaz lay to sleep, to uncover his feet after he was asleep and to lie at his feet. Ruth obeyed. Boaz awoke during the night and discovered a woman at his feet. He blessed her and told her that he knew she was a virtuous woman (Vs 11). He knew that there was a kinsman that should have first choice for Ruth. He went to meet with that man at the gate. He took ten elders with him. Boaz told the man that Naomi had a field to sell AND a widowed daughter-in-law that would go with the purchase of the field. The man told Boaz that he would not buy the field and therefore have Ruth because he was afraid that this would mess up his inheritance. The man took off his shoe and gave it to Boaz in testimony of this agreement. That freed Boaz to buy the field and to marry Ruth. Ruth gave birth to Obed who became the grandfather of David. Therefore, Ruth became a part of the ancestry of JESUS!!! Is this the first book of the Bible so far without wars, whining, complaining and outright sin?

The REAL love story of Ruth points us to Jesus—THE GREAT REDEEMER.

LESSON NINE

FIRST SAMUEL

Classified as a historical Book of the Bible.

Chapter 1: Elkanah had two wives. One wife, Hannah, was barren. She wanted a son so badly that she promised God that she would give him back to God. She prayed so hard that Eli, the high priest, thought that she was drunk. When he realized that she was praying, he asked that God give her the petition of her heart. Did he know then that he would be blessed with Samuel? Samuel was born to Elkanah and Hannah. When he was weaned, she took Samuel to the temple and loaned him back to God as she had promised. She told Eli that Samuel was the answer to her prayer. Was this the first baby dedication?

Chapter 2: Vss 1–10: Hannah's Prayer and Praise time. Vs 11: Samuel was left at the temple. Vss 12–16: Eli's sons were evil. Eli knew this but did not attempt to discipline them. See Vs 22. None of Eli's family would live to be old. See Vs 32.

Chapter 3: We all know the story of Samuel's call. Three times God called him and Samuel ran to Eli. The third time Eli realized that it was God calling Samuel and so he told Samuel to go lie down again and that God would call again. This time God came to Samuel and talked to him. Vss 10–14: Samuel told Eli what God had told him. Eli accepted the message.

Chapter 4: The Philistines were winning the battle against the Israelites until the Ark of the Covenant was brought into the camp. Then the Philistines were afraid but 30,000 Israelites, including Eli's two sons, were killed in one day. Eli was ninety-eight years old. When he heard that Phineas and Hophni were dead, he fell off his seat, broke his neck and died. Ever wonder where the word Ichabod originated? Ichabod means the spirit of God has departed/the glory is gone/there is no glory. See First Samuel Chapter 4, Verses 21 & 22 as Ichabod's mother declared "the glory is departed from Israel".

Chapter 23: David's farewell speech. Even though David sinned, he loved God. Remember First Samuel 16:13. God's spirit remained on David. Don't let the Devil defeat you when you sin. The battle is the Lord's—in our lives as believers as well as in the days of the Old Testament!

Chapter 24: There was a census taken. For nine months and twenty days, Joab and his leaders counted. There were 800,000 men in Israel and there were 500,000 men in Judah. God offered David three things: 1). Seven years of famine; 2). To run from the enemy for three months; 3). Three days of pestilence. The pestilence came. David bought a threshing floor and offered burnt offerings and peace offerings. What a sad and tragic end to the reign of a great king. What was David's downfall?

LESSON ELEVEN
FIRST AND SECOND KINGS

FIRST KINGS

Just like the name, these two books talk about the line of kings after David. Israel had split into two nations and became the Northern Kingdom (Israel) and the Southern kingdom (Judah). Ten tribes comprised Israel and two tribes comprised Judah. Samaria was the capital of Israel and Jerusalem (the city of David) was the capital of Judah. Remember this as we study further the ancestry of Jesus. POINT TO PONDER: With the split into two nations, did the Covenant change?

Chapter 1: Adonijah, a son of David and Haggith, decided that he wanted to be king. Joab, David's general, helped him. Joab knew that Solomon was anointed to be king. Was this a political move on his part? We see multiple times throughout these two books that Joab is a troublemaker. Nathan, the prophet, told Bathsheba that Adonijah was preparing for the kingship. He knew that David had promised it to Solomon. Vs 30: David assured that Solomon was to be King. Vs 39: Solomon was anointed king by Zadok the priest. The people rejoiced. Adonijah was afraid. David told him that if there was no evil in him, he would be safe. Was Adonijah able to refrain from evil?

Chapter 2: David instructed Solomon to follow the Lord. Vs 10: David was buried in the City of David. Was this Bethlehem (where he was born) or Jerusalem (where he reigned)? Read Second Samuel 5: 7–9. Vs 25: Solomon had Adonijah killed.

Chapter 3: Solomon made an alliance with Pharaoh and married his daughter. Solomon knew this was wrong. God had told his people many times, not to intermarry because of the dangers of turning from God and worshipping idols. Vs 3: How could Solomon love God and worship idols (high places)? Vs 9: Solomon asked God for wisdom and the wisdom to know the difference between good and evil. Vss 10–14: God gave him great wisdom. Read the familiar story in Vss 16–28 about the two mothers and their sons.

Chapter 4: Solomon was king over all Israel but Judah remained a separate kingdom. We are given a view of some of Solomon's wealth in this chapter. Vs 26 tells us that he had 40,000 horse stalls and 12,000 horsemen. Vs 34: People came from all over the known world to hear Solomon's wisdom and to see the great wealth and beauty of his lands and buildings.

Chapter 5: Solomon hired Hiram, the king of Tyre, to build the temple. They used Cedars and firs of Lebanon and precious stones.

Chapter 6: 480 years after the exodus, Solomon started the temple. It was built ninety feet long by thirty feet wide and forty five feet tall. Vss 11–13: God tells Solomon to walk in God's ways and to obey His laws. IF Solomon obeyed and walked upright in God's sight, God would bless him and Israel. Vs 22: The whole temple was overlaid with Gold. Vs 38 tells us that it took seven years to build it.

Chapter 7: Solomon spent seven years building the temple but thirteen years building his own house. His house was 150' Long x 75' Wide x 45' tall. Who was important to Solomon? God or himself?

Chapter 8: The Ark of the Covenant was brought to the temple. First Kings Chapter 8, Verse 11 tells us "the glory of the Lord had filled the house of the Lord".

Chapter 9: God reminded Solomon again to walk uprightly.

Chapter 10: The Queen of Sheba went to visit Solomon to see the beauty of the temple and to hear Solomon's wisdom. She was amazed at both. Vs 14: $3.83 BILLION of gold was added to Solomon's wealth in one year. Vs 23: Solomon was noted to be the most wealthy and the wisest king. Vs 29: He bought a chariot for $76,000 and a horse for $19,200!

Chapter 11: Solomon loved women. He loved women from many countries. God had told him not to intermarry because they would turn him away from God. Read Second Corinthians 6: 14–18 for a New Testament teaching. Vs 3 states that Solomon had 700 wives and princesses as well as 300 concubines. Surely enough: Vs 9 tells us that Solomon turned away from God. God was angry. Vss 42–43 say that Solomon reigned forty years and died as a young man. First Kings 3:7 said that Solomon considered himself a child when he became king. He, too, was buried in the City of David.

Chapter 12: Rehoboam—Solomon's son—became king. Vs 28: He built two golden calves for the people to worship. Also in this chapter we see the split into two kingdoms. Read carefully as we see Jeroboam and Rehoboam. Rehoboam was king over Judah and Jeroboam was king over Israel.

Chapter 13: Vss 33–34 Jeroboam did not turn back to God.

Chapter 14: More ungodly kings.

Chapter 15: Vs 6: War between Jeroboam and Rehoboam all their days. Vs 9: Asa became king over Judah for forty-one years. He was a righteous king.

Chapter 16: More evil kings of Israel. Vs 29 introduced Ahab, an evil king. He married Jezebel. Vs 33 says that he did more to provoke the Lord to anger than all the kings of Israel before him.

Chapter 17: Introduction to Elijah, the Tishbite. God told him that there would be no rain. God sent him to rest by the brook Cherith where the ravens fed him. Vs 9: God sent Elijah to a widow. Elijah asked her for bread and water. The widow had very little, but Elijah told her that god would provide. Her son got sick and died. Elijah prayed over the son and he lived again.

Chapter 18: Elijah versus Ahab. Elijah was the only prophet of God at that time. Baal had 450 prophets. Two bullocks were killed and cut up and placed on the wood of the altar. Elijah told the prophets of Baal to call on their gods to send fire. They called on their gods all morning and no fire fell. At noon, Elijah mocked them saying that maybe their gods were asleep. They cried and cut themselves to get the attention of their gods. That evening, Elijah built an altar of twelve stones, put the wood on it and then cut up a bullock on the wood. They poured four barrels of water over the bullock and wood. Three times they poured barrels of water over the bullock. Elijah prayed to God and the fire fell. It consumed everything, even the stones. Elijah had the 450 prophets of Baal killed. Elijah told Ahab to get ready for rain after more than three years of drought. The rain came!

Chapter 19: Jezebel threatened to kill Elijah. He went into the wilderness and sat under a Juniper tree and begged God to let him die. Instead, God gave him food and water. However, Elijah continued his pity party. God gave him instructions to go anoint kings and to anoint Elisha to be the next prophet. He threw his mantle over Elisha. Elisha ministered to Elijah.

Chapter 20: War between Syria and Israel.

Chapter 21: Ahab wanted Naboth's vineyard. Naboth refused. Remember that Ahab was evil and the husband of an evil woman- Jezebel. Jezebel decided she would get that vineyard, so she ordered Naboth to be stoned. God sent Elijah to Ahab to tell him that the dogs would lick up the blood where he had Naboth killed. He also told him that dogs would eat Jezebel.

Chapter 22: Three years of war between Syria and Israel.

SECOND KINGS

Chapter 1: How did Ahaziah describe Elijah Vs 8: What happened to the fifty-one men (Vs 10)? What happened to the second group of fifty-one men (Vs 12)? Did the same thing happen to the third group of fifty-one men?

Chapter 2: Where did Elisha follow Elijah in Vss 2, 4, 6? In Vs 8 we read that the Jordan parted again. What did Elisha request from Elijah in Vs 9? What a compliment to Elijah. Vs 11: A chariot of fire, horses of fire and a whirlwind. Elijah was taken up to heaven in the whirlwind. Did Elisha see him taken up (Vs 12)? Do we ever see or hear from Elijah after he is taken to heaven? Read Malachi 4:5, Matthew 17:3 and Revelations chapter 11. Vs 14: The Jordan parted yet again. Vs 19: What problem did the people of Jericho have? How did God fix that problem? Read Vss 20–22. Vss 23, 24 tell about some irreverent kids that mocked Elisha as a bald man. What happened to them?

Chapter 3: God's irrigation system. The people did not see wind and did not see rain but the valley was made full of water for human consumption, for the animals and for the crops (Vss 16–20). Vs 27 tells the horrible news of the King of Moab offering his son as a burnt offering.

Chapter 4: The miracle of oil to pay a debt in Vss 1–7. Beginning in Vs 8, we read about a woman of Shunem that invited Elisha for a meal and then set up a room for him. She was blessed with a son. The boy died. She rode hard to find Elisha when the boy died. Vs 34: The first CPR? Vss 39–44: Feeding the people.

Chapter 5: Naaman was commander in chief of the Syrian army. He became a leper. A little girl told his wife about Elisha. Elisha told Naaman to wash in the Jordan River seven times. Naaman got mad and tried to leave but his servants encouraged him to try it. Naaman was healed! Elisha refused payment. Vss 20–27: What did greed and deception cost?

Chapter 6:

A borrowed ox

A worried man

Will iron float?

This ax head can.

Read about it in Second Kings

Chapter 6 has interesting things.

God's army rides in chariots of fire

They filled the mountain all around

The likes of which are not for hire

When GOD fights your battles, miracles abound

Read all about it in Second Kings

Chapter 6—what interesting things.

There was a great famine in Samaria's land

One pint of dove dung cost five pieces of silver

The king of Israel boiled his own son

Then went looking for Elisha to behead him.

Chapter 7: The high price of flour. Four lepers invaded the Syrian camp and found plenty food

and drink, along with silver, gold and clothing.

Chapter 8: More kings. Did any of them follow God?

Chapter 9: What does it mean to drive like Jehu (Vs 20)? What is meant by painted up like a Jezebel (Vs 30)? What happened to Jezebel? Did this fulfill Elijah's prophecy in First Kings 21:23 and Vss 30–37?

Chapter 10: Ahab had seventy sons. Ahab was Jezebel's husband. See First Kings 19: 16, 17. Jehu was to destroy the descendants of Ahab. Also see Second Kings 9:4–10. Jehu destroyed Baal in Vs 28 but he did not follow God (Vs 31).

Chapter 11: Does Vs 1 say that this woman killed her own children? A woman ruler? Vs 3 tells us that she ruled over the land. Is that why she killed the children? To prevent them from getting in the way of her politics? When I read this, it sounds so much like today. Vs 14 sounds like some women of our time who have exalted themselves in the US Government crying TREASON. Vs 16 tells us what happened to her. Jehoida, the priest, made a covenant with God. He destroyed the altars and images of Baal. A child king? Vs 21 tells us that Jehoash was seven years old when he began to reign.

Chapter 12: The child king Jehoash (Joash) reigned for forty years. Finally a king who did right in the sight of God. Vss 4–9 talk about money being raised to repair the House of the Lord. Vs 9: Was this the first piggy bank? The first building fund?

Chapter 13: Elisha died. See Vs 14.

Chapter 14: Why is it important to destroy idols and the places of idol worship? Exodus 20:4 tells us not to have any graven images. Deuteronomy 7:5 said to destroy the altars, to break the images, to cut down the groves and to burn them with fire. Vss 3, 4 show that he did not destroy the places of idol worship even though Vs 3 says that he followed God in other ways. Read 12: 2, 3 and read 17: 9. What happens when they are destroyed? Second Kings 18:3–7, Second Kings 23:3–6, Second Kings 17:3–6.

Chapter 15: A sixteen year old king reigned for fifty-two years. Vss 3, 4: He did right in the sight of God but he did not remove the places of idol worship. This chapter lists more evil kings.

Chapter 16: More evil kings

Chapter 17: More evil kings. Vs 13, 14: God told them to turn from their evil ways but they rejected God.

Chapter 18: At last! There is HOPE. Vs 3- 5: Hezekiah followed God. He got rid of the idols. What a compliment in Vs 5. It says he trusted God.

Chapter 19: We meet Isaiah. Isaiah told Hezekiah not to be afraid. Vs 19: Hezekiah took the letter from Isaiah to the House of the Lord and interceded with God.

Chapter 20: Hezekiah was sick. Isaiah told him to put his house in order. He turned his face to the wall and prayed. Vss 4–11: He got a sign from God.

Chapter 21: A twelve year old king. Evil. More evil kings.

Chapter 22: Josiah, the eight year old king, did right in the sight of God. Vs 8 tells us that the high priest found the Book of the Law while repairing the House of the Lord.

Chapter 23: The king read the Book of the Law to the people. They cleaned the idols out of the House of the Lord and burned them. Josiah restored the Passover.

Chapter 24: Remember Nebuchadnezzar? He was King of Babylon.

Chapter 25: The House of the Lord was ransacked. The furnishings were destroyed or stolen. The city was devastated. Everyone RAN BACK TO EGYPT.

LESSON TWELVE
FIRST AND SECOND CHRONICLES

What are Chronicles? A factual, written account of events in the order of occurrence. A timeline.

These Chronicles only review Judah (the Southern Kingdom).

FIRST CHRONICLES

Chapter 1: A list of the descendants of Adam and some of the Kings. When we add Vss 1–27 to Matthew 1:1–16, we can trace from Adam to Jesus. Also, read Luke3:23–38.

Chapters 2 & 3: More lineage.

Chapter 4: The Prayer of Jabez (means sorrow). Are we brave enough to pray this prayer?

Chapter 5: More wars. Vs 22 says the war was of GOD.

Chapters 6–9: More genealogies. A great review.

Chapter 10: A replay of the war with the Philistines and of Saul's death.

Chapters 11–29: A great review of David's reign. Chapter 16: 8-–36 is a Psalm of Praise.

SECOND CHRONICLES

Chapter 1: A review of the reign of Solomon.

Chapters 2–5: A review of building the temple and placing the Ark of the Covenant in the temple.

Chapter 6: A speech and a prayer of Solomon.

Chapter 7: Read Vss 12–14. Does this apply to today?

Chapter 8: A warning. Solomon would not let his wife (a daughter of Pharaoh) live in the house of David.

Chapter 9: The Queen of Sheba came to visit. She was amazed at the wealth, wisdom and beauty of Solomon and his land. A review of the great wealth of Solomon.

Chapter 10: The nation of Israel divided into two kingdoms.

Chapter 11: Vs 4: God told Rehoboam and the kingdom of Judah not to fight the Northern Kingdom of Israel. Vs 13: The Levites moved to Judah. Vs 16: Other people of the Northern Kingdom moved to the Southern Kingdom.

Chapter 12: The Egyptians raided Jerusalem.

Chapter 13: War between the kingdoms. Vss 16–18: God delivered Judah.

Chapter 14: Remember ASA from First Kings 15? Vs 2 says that he did right in the sight of God. He cleaned up the idolatry.

Chapters 15–36: Kings and more kings. There were twenty kings of Judah. This is a continuing review of First and Second Kings.

LESSON THIRTEEN
Ezra, Nehemiah, Haggai, Zechariah, Malachi

These post captivity prophets encouraged the rebuilding of Jerusalem and the Temple

At this point we will study these post-captivity prophets even though they are not in this order in the Bible.

EZRA:

Chapter 1: Vss 1–3: Why are these verses familiar? Read Second Chronicles 36:21–23. Ezra was a prophet who led the return of one of the remnants of the Israelite nation after seventy years of exile in Babylon. Vs 2 tells us that Cyrus ruled the whole earth. He ordered the rebuilding of the temple in Jerusalem (Vs. 7). Even the furnishings that Nebuchadnezzar had stolen from the temple earlier were taken back to Jerusalem to be restored to the Temple.

Chapter 2: An accounting of the people and the animals.

Chapter 3: Vss 1–6: Sacrifices and burnt offerings were made even before the Temple was built. Remember when Solomon ordered Cedars of Lebanon to build the Temple? More were ordered for the rebuilding of the Temple. Vss 10, 11 tell about the praise and worship when the foundation was laid. Vs 12: The older people were upset because the rebuilt Temple did not measure up to the earlier one.

Chapter 4: There was interference with the construction. Artaxerxes ordered the construction to halt. Why? Loss of revenue for the government. Sound familiar?

Chapter 5: Once again, the people were asked who had told them to build the Temple and to rebuild the wall (Vss 5:13 and 1:2).

Chapter 6: Proof that Cyrus made the decree was found in the king's treasure house. Also, they found the order for the vessels and the furnishings to be restored. He ordered those who previously tried to interfere to help AND to provide the animals for the sacrifices. Read Vss 11, 12. Vss 19–22: The Children of Israel kept the Passover.

Chapter 7: How good is your math? What kin was Ezra to Aaron (of Moses and Aaron) (Vss 1–5)? How did Artaxerxes feel about Ezra? How long was the journey from Babylon to Jerusalem (Vs 9)? (4 months). What was Ezra's mission in Vs 10?

Chapter 8: A genealogy – a counting of those who left Babylon during the reign of Artaxerxes.

Chapter 9: The people continued to intermarry. This astonished Ezra. Vss 3–6.

Chapter 10: Sin exposed. A listing of the men who had intermarried. Nothing is hidden from God.

NEHEMIAH:

Chapter 1: Nehemiah was a government employee. He lived at Shusan, the palace where Ahasureus reigned over 127 provinces. He was a cupholder for the king. Vs 4 states that Nehemiah wept, mourned, fasted, and prayed over the children of Israel.

Chapter 2: Vs 5 tells us that Nehemiah was a godly man. Vss 2–8 state that he had prayed, fasted, wept, mourned until his looks changed and Ahasureus noticed this. Ahasureus asked Nehemiah what was wrong. Nehemiah told Ahasureus about his burden and his calling from God. Ahasureus gave him letters to allow him to travel safely back to Jerusalem to build the wall. Why build a wall? How many gates? Why so many gates? Read on to learn.

Chapter 3: Families built sections of the wall at the same time. The wall was about two and one-half miles long, forty feet high and eight feet wide. According to Nehemiah 6:15, the wall was finished in fifty- two days. Some of the gates were not completed by that point, but the wall itself was done. How many gates were there in this wall? A great lesson in working together.

Chapter 4: Enemies scoffed at the folks building the wall. Vss 4, 5: Nehemiah prayed. Vs 7: The enemies got madder. Vs 9: Nehemiah continued to pray and set up watchmen day and night. Vs 23: They even slept in their workclothes—ready to work or ready to fight. Compassion for their job.

Chapter 5: Vs 6: Nehemiah was angry. Why? Because the rich oppressed the poor. This concept continues today, many years later. Vs 11: Nehemiah told the rich to return the money and land to the oppressed. Vs 12: The land and money were restored. Vs 14: Nehemiah became Governor of Judah for twelve years.

Chapter 6: Four times Sanballat sent for Nehemiah. (Sounds a bit like the time Satan tried to tempt Jesus in the wilderness.) These were schemes to get Nehemiah in a situation where Sanballat could kill him.

Chapter 7: A census of the children of Israel who had come up out of captivity in Babylon.

Chapter 8: Ezra read the Book of the Law of Moses from morning to midday. The people listened! Vs 5 says that the people stood for the reading (maybe five hours or so). Would we do that today? We don't usually stand for a five minute reading of the scriptures. Vs 6: A praise service. The people bowed their faces to the ground to honor God. They were so blessed to hear God's word (Vs 9) that they cried. Vs 10: Was this dinner on the grounds? Vss 13–18: Feast of the Booths. They made the booths out of gathered tree limbs and branches. Ezra read every day for seven days. The eight day was the Assembly.

Chapter 9: The Children of Israel fasted and prayed and read God's Word and confessed their sins. The rest of the chapter is a recap of history from Adam to their time. God's mercy shone through.

Chapter 10: A list of those making agreement (oath) to walk in God's law.

Chapter 11: Those who lived in Jerusalem and those who lived outside the wall. It appears that many people preferred to live outside the wall.

Chapter 12: The list of workers in preparation for the dedication of the wall. Vs 43 says that the people rejoiced so loudly that they were heard far away.

Chapter 13: Nehemiah was grieved that the people had not stayed true to God. He ordered a cleansing of the chambers and that the vessels be brought back into the House of the Lord.

NOTE: Now we skip to Haggai, Zechariah and Malachi—prophets in the same era as Ezra and Nehemiah.

HAGGAI:

Chapter 1: Vs 6: Haggai told the people that they worked and worked but were never satisfied. Have times changed? Vss 7,8: He told them to go gather wood and build the House of the Lord. Vs 11: Drought.

Chapter 2: Remember Zerubbabel from Ezra chapter 2? He led the first remnant home from Babylon. Vss 6, 7: God promised to shake the earth and fill the House of the Lord with GLORY. Vs 9: The glory of the latter house will outshine the former. He also promised peace. Read Hebrews 12:25–29.

ZECHARIAH:

Another post captivity prophet. He was also a priest. He had visions. My best theory is that the Book of Zechariah is full of prophecies, even prophecies of Jesus.

Chapter 1: Zechariah saw a man riding a red horse through the myrtle. Does this speak of the judgment? Vss 14, 15 say that God is jealous FOR Jerusalem and Zion. He dearly loves them and wants them to return to Him.

Chapter 2: A vision of a man with a measuring line. Vs 4: Jerusalem to be inhabited as towns without walls. Does that mean that Jerusalem will outgrow its walls? Vs 6: Is this a prophecy of the Jews being scattered throughout many countries?

Chapter 3: Vs 3 speaks of filthy garments. Sin? Unrighteousness? IS Vs 8 a prophecy of Jesus?

Zechariah Chapter 4, Verse 6 says "Not by might, not by power, but by my spirit saith the Lord of hosts.

Chapters 5, 6: More prophecies.

Chapter 7: Vss 8, 9: God spoke to Zechariah to execute true judgment and to show mercy and compassion. Vs 10: Good words for now. Do not oppress, don't think evil of your brother. Vss 11–14: The scattering of the Jews to many lands due to refusing to hear God.

Chapter 8: God said that Jerusalem will be inhabited again with young and old. Is this a prophecy of the restoration of Israel in 1948 OR is this a prophecy of Christ's return? Vs 12: God blessed and prospered everything. Vs 22: Prophecy of the modern day tourism of the Holy Land?

Chapter 9: Vs 9: King riding a lowly beast? Is this Jesus's triumphal entry into Jerusalem on Palm Sunday?

Chapter 10: The latter rain. Blessings? Vs 5 sounds like some of the modern day wars that Israel has fought. A small nation, but mighty in warfare.

Chapter 11: More prophecy.

Chapter 12: Vs 9: WATCH YOUR STEP!!! Read and re-read this verse. If we do not get anything else out of this study in Zechariah, UNDERSTAND THIS VERSE.

Chapter 13: Vs 7 says that if you smite the shepherd, the sheep are scattered. Remember all the times that the Children of Israel fell away from God on the excuse that there was no leader? Is this still true with us today?

Chapter 14: GOD WILL FIGHT FOR ISRAEL. What a promise!!!!

MALACHI

Chapter 1: Vs 1 refers to this message as a burden. Vs 2: God loves us but that love is not always returned. Vs 11: God was rejected by the Children of Israel, so His love was offered to the Gentiles. This is fulfilled in Acts. What are we, the Gentiles, doing to Him today?

Chapter 2: Curses.

Chapter 3: Vs 1: Is this a reference to John the Baptist? Vs 8: The people were (are) robbing God of tithes and offerings. Vs 9: They (we?) are cursed for robbing God. Vs 10: Blessings for tithing.

Chapter 4: Fear of God brings blessings and growth. Vs 5: Elijah will be sent before the Great and Dreadful Day of the Lord. Vs 6: Fathers will love their children. Children will love their fathers. Or God will send a curse on the world. Did you know that the last thing in the Old Testament is about this curse?

LESSON FOURTEEN
ESTHER

THE RIGHT PERSON AT THE RIGHT TIME

The Book of Esther was written during the time of Ezra and Nehemiah. See the reference to King Ahasureus.

Chapter 1: Vs 4: A party that lasted 180 days. Vs 5: Seven more days of a party for the lesser folks. Vss 6–8: No expenses spared. Gold, Silver, lots of alcohol. Vs 9: Vashti was queen and made a feast for the females. Vss 10 –13: Ahasureus ordered Vashti to stand before him to show off her beauty. She refused and he got angry. The wise men devised a plan to keep women under control and to demand them to honor their husbands, that men would rule.

Chapter 2: These men recommended that all the fair young maidens be brought to the king for review. The one that pleased the king would become Queen. Mordecai was a Jew brought into captivity by Nebuchadnezzar. He worked in Shushan. He brought his cousin Esther to be in the review. He had raised her after her parents died. The keeper of the women liked her and gave her seven maids. For six months she received treatments of oil of Myrrh and then six more months of sweet odours and other purifications. She had her visit to the king. She became Queen. Vs 18: Another feast in preparation. Vss 21–23: 2 men wanted to kill King Ahasureus. Mordecia learned this. He told Esther and she told the king. The two men were hanged.

Chapter 3: Haman got a promotion above all the princes. Mordecai refused to bow to him. Haman wanted to destroy all the Jews. A decree was made to kill all the Jews, young and old, in one day.

Chapter 4: Mordecai put on sackcloth and ashes. Esther sent him clothes, but he refused to give up the sackcloth. He sent word to Esther of the decree to destroy the Jews. He did not want anyone to know they were kin and that she was a Jewess. Vs14: Esther was placed in the palace by God for just such a time. She asked Mordecai to gather the people to fast and pray for three days.

Chapter 5: On the third day of prayer and fasting, she went to visit the king. He held out the golden scepter to her. She told him that she was preparing a banquet for the king and for Haman. Read Vss 5–13 about Haman's pride and anger. His wife told him to build a gallows. He had it built.

Chapter 6: The king couldn't sleep so he read. He read about the plot to kill him and that Mordecai had spoiled that plot. He wanted to honor Mordecai. He gave him royal robes and his personal horse and a crown.

Chapter 7: Finally—the banquet! Esther revealed Haman's plan. The king got mad and went out to the garden. Haman fell upon Esther's bed. The king had him hanged on the very gallows that Haman had built for Mordecai.

Chapter 8: Esther got Haman's house. Mordecai received the king's ring. Esther asked the king to reverse the death sentence of the Jews. The Jews were saved.

Chapter 9: Purim is a word from Pur which is the casting of lots. Purim is still celebrated from this origin. Vss 13, 14: Haman's ten sons were hanged also.

Chapter 10: Mordecai became Second in Command. QUESTION: How many times is God mentioned in the Book of Esther?

LESSON FIFTEEN

JOB

I have no idea when Job was written. Today, we still call people Job when a lot of unusual things happen to them.

Chapter 1: Vs 1: Job was perfect and upright. Let me write that again. Job was PERFECT and UPRIGHT. Vs 3: He had great wealth. Vs 7: Satan WAS and IS real. He still roams the earth. Revelations 12:10 says he is the accuser of the brethren. Job 1:10: There was a hedge around Job and his house and all that he had. Psalms 91:11–12: God limits Satan by giving his angels charge over us to keep us and to bear us up. Job 1:13–19: Job's children partied while 1000 oxen and 500 asses were stolen, the servants were killed by the Sabeans, the fire burned up 7000 sheep. 3000 camels were stolen. Then his sons were killed by a great wind. What kind of man was Job (Vss 21–22)?

Chapter 2: Boils. Vs 9: Job received bad advice from his wife. She told him to curse God and die. Then three friends showed up. Has anyone ever come on the pretense of comforting you and supporting you (but actually made things worse)? Example: A family member has just been diagnosed with a terminal disease and some stranger calls to talk to you about all the horrors of chemo and treatments that their relative suffered? Or maybe someone uses your time of sorrow to whine and describe their pains and problems in great detail. This is how I see these so-called friends. This is more reason to choose our friends wisely. These guys sat on the ground for seven days and seven nights and didn't talk, but then, they started talking and judging Job and giving terrible advice.

Chapter 3: Job's speech. He cursed the day he was born.

Chapters 4, 5: Eliphaz's speech.

Chapters 6, 7: Job spoke.

Chapter 8: BIldad's speech.

Chapters 9, 10: Job spoke.

Chapter 11: Zophar's speech.

Chapters 12–14: Job answered.

Chapter 15: Eliphaz spoke again.

Chapters 16, 17: Job spoke.

Chapter 18: Bildad spoke again.

Chapter 19: Job spoke again.

Chapter 20: Zophar spoke.

Chapter 21: Job spoke again.

Chapter 22: Eliaphaz again.

Chapters 23, 24: Job spoke again.

Chapter 25: Bildad spoke again.

Chapters 26–31: Job spoke at length.

Chapters 32–37: Argument among friends. A fourth friend appeared.

Chapters 38, 39: God spoke to Job. These are SCIENCE chapters with lots of questions to ponder.

Chapter 40: God spoke to Job again.

Chapter 41: God put Job on the spot by asking questions.

Chapter 42: Job answered God. God spoke to the friends in Vss 7–9. Vss 12–16: God blessed Job again. Vs 17 tells us that Job died at 210 years of age. (Seventy years were before he lost everything but God and 140 years after restoration.)

LESSON SIXTEEN
BOOK OF PSALMS

The Book of Psalms is a book of Hymns, a book of poetry. There are 150 Psalms in this book. The longest one is Psalm 119. The shortest one is Psalm 117. There are several authors, including King David. These chapters vary from songs of praise and thanksgiving to cries from the depths of desperate hearts.

Many of us can quote Psalm 23. Some can even quote Psalm 100 and others. These are not just a one-time read. Mark your favorites and read them when you need them.

Blessed means happy. We see this word many times in the Book of Psalms. As early as Psalm 2:7, we see prophecies of Jesus. I will share a few with you as we go, but there are many more.

Psalm 22:1 states the words of Jesus on the cross. How many references about Jesus can you find in chapter 22? Vs 1, 7, 8, 16, 18, 20, 22.

Read chapter 24 and answer the questions in Vs 3. The answer is in Vs 4.

Having trouble sleeping? Read Psalm 4. MEMORIZE Vs 8. During a very troubled time, I would repeat this as I went to bed. I slept!

Selah may mean forever, or it may indicate the end of a thought.

Psalm 27: What is David's desire (Vs 4)?

Psalm 37 is a book of instructions. Vs 1: Don't fret or be envious; Psalm Chapter 37, Verse 3 says "Trust in the Lord, and do good"; Vs 4 tells us to delight (joy) in the Lord; Vs 5: Follow God and trust in Him; Psalm Chapter 37, Verse 7 says "Rest in the Lord, and wait patiently for him, fret not".

Psalm Chapter 37, Verse 8 says" Cease from anger, and forsake wrath, fret not thyself in any wise to do evil". Psalm Chapter 37, Verse 34 says "Wait on the Lord, and keep his way".

Psalm 46: A Psalm for current times. God is our Help. He is always ready to help us in times of trouble. We are certainly a troubled people right now, but God is in control.

Psalm 78: A review of the exodus.

Psalm 90: How old is God? Vs 10: How long do we live?

Psalm 91 talks about protection.

Who is Asaph? He is credited with writing some of the Psalms. He was more than likely a Levite and appointed by King David to lead singing. He wrote his own songs.

Remember the Covenant that God made with Abraham? Read Psalm 105 & 106. This is a review of the time from Abraham to Canaan. That time must have been important to receive several reviews in the Bible.

Psalm 107: Give thanks. Claim your redemption and say I am redeemed. For what do you hunger and thirst? Cry out to God. He will deliver you. Remember the Israelites? They wandered in the wilderness for forty years. God took them to a land of milk and honey. Both of these are good for us physically. I just read an article about honey and learned that it does not rot unless it becomes contaminated. It contains antioxidants, has healing powers for burns and bed sores as well as other wounds. It contains various of the Vitamin B class. (God's humor! B Vitamins come from Bees?)

America is basically a land of milk and honey. We have been SO blessed. So blessed that other countries are jealous and want to destroy us. But wait. It is not just other countries that want to destroy America and the Christian faith. There are people within our own borders, citizens and non-citizens as well, that are working to destroy America and to destroy Christians in particular. These are people with great (unimaginable) financial wealth, with many years of formal education, with leadership roles in our government. God help us. We MUST wake up. We must pray without ceasing. We must remain strong.

Read Psalm 107. It tells us what to do. We are to praise God, to claim our redemption, to trust in God. Remember folks, Covid-19 is not the enemy. The murdering hornets that have suddenly appeared in the Western part of America have given rise to more fear in addition to the Covid-19 virus. Who brought them to America? Why are they in America? The large news media tell us that an entire Honey Bee colony can be destroyed by just one of these hornets if it gets into the hive. Think about that. Does that sound like an enemy that we fight daily? The enemy is much bigger than any man-made virus. SIN is the enemy. The sin of corruption and greed and ungodliness. So many people are afraid, so afraid that fear dominates every move and every thought. Yes, Covid-19 is serious and it can kill. But look at the abortion industry. How many lives are destroyed every day in America due to abortion? Look at the murders each day. Yes. SIN is the problem and there is a cure. The cure is JESUS CHRIST. Thank you, Jesus, for being the cure. How do you get this cure? Dust off your Bibles and READ them. PRAY. Prepare yourselves to be delivered from fear and sin. God will deliver. He is faithful. Read Psalm 107 until you fully grasp that GOD is our REDEEMER.

Psalm 111:10: What is the beginning of wisdom? 113:3 How long are we to praise God?

Distressed? Fearful? Read Psalm 121. Psalm 136: How long does God's mercy endure?

Psalm 150: PRAISE!!!! EVERYTHING that breathes should PRAISE THE LORD!

LESSON SEVENTEEN
PROVERBS

Written by Solomon, a son of King David. Solomon was known as the wisest man in the world—a gift from God. What is the beginning of wisdom? Read 1:7. 2:1–5 lists the eight things that are required to understand the fear of the Lord. 3:5,6,11,12 address correction and discipline. Read 14:12; 16:25; 17:22; 18:21; 22: 1, 6. Proverbs contrast wise and foolish, workers vs lazy people, riches vs poverty.

LESSON EIGHTEEN
ECCLESIASTES

Means preacher. Was written by Solomon. Chapter 1 sounds a lot like Proverbs. Vanity (emptiness) is the main theme. Chapter 2: Solomon describes his wealth and desires but states that this is all in vain. Vs 15 tells us that even his great wisdom was vanity. Chapter 3: There is a season (time) for everything. Vs 17 says there is even a time for God to judge. Chapter 4 talks about oppression and depression. Vss 8–12: Two working together are better than one alone. Chapter 5: Vs 14 tells us to pay what we promise/pledge. Vs 15 says that we entered the world naked and we will leave this old world with Nothing. Chapter 6: Our appetites are never satisfied. Chapter 7: Your good name is better than riches. Vs 7: There is NO human on earth that has not sinned. Chapter 8: We don't have the final say. Chapter 9: Vs 10 tells us to give our best. Chapters 10 and 11: More Proverbs. Chapter 12 Vss 13 and 14: What is man's duty?

LESSON NINETEEN
SONG OF SOLOMON

Written by Solomon. A Love Poem. Many commentaries state that this is about God and His love for the church. There are many sensory references in this book. Vs 3: Savour (a pleasant smell or taste). Vss 10, 11: Our eyes see jewelry. Vs 12: Spikenard—an expensive ointment. Read Luke 7:37–39; Mark 14:3–8; John 12:1–8. Vs 13 talks about Myrrh. We are familiar with this both in the birth and death of Jesus. Read John 19:39, 40; Luke 23:56; Matthew 2:11. Vs 14: We are familiar with Camphor which we use as an analgesic. It is aromatic and is currently used in essential oils. Chapter 2: Spring time and growth. Do we normally see apple trees growing in a forest? The apple tree gives food and some fluid to the animal population. This chapter also points out the uniqueness of the Bride of Christ. Chapter 3: The bride seeks the bridegroom. The wedding bed was perfumed with myrrh and frankincense. Vs 7 tells us that it took sixty men to carry the marriage bed. There is a description of the marriage bed in Vss 8–10. Chapter 4: A beautiful description of the bride and her perfection. The groom cannot take his eyes off of her. (Thank you Lord, that you never turn away from us.) Vss 12–15 talks about a garden of herbs and perfumes. Vs 16: The wind was requested to come and blow the fragrances around. Chapter 5: The bride was searching for the bridegroom. According to Vs 8, she is lovesick. Are we lovesick for God? Do we search diligently for him? The bride describes the beauty and perfection and strength of the bridegroom. The New Testament tells us that Jesus did not have physical appearances that would make someone search for Him as an earthy lover, but we all should desire Him.

LESSON TWENTY

ISAIAH

Written by Isaiah. What is a prophet? A person who speaks for God. A spokesperson. See Exodus 7:1: Aaron was Moses's prophet (spokesperson). Deuteronomy 18:22 tells us how to know a true prophet for God. As we move into the study of the prophets, we will see a lot of repetition. God gave the Children of Israel so many chances to turn back to God, but they were too involved in the world of sin and idol worship. At first, we might be inclined to criticize these folks, but how long has God been working with us and we still see so much sin today? These books of prophecy are not necessarily written in chronological order. They were all written before the birth of Christ.

Chapter 1: Vs 1 sets a time line of the kings of Judah. Vs 3 tells us that God's people had rebelled and turned against God to the point that they didn't know God. Does Vs 4 sound like current times? Vs 5 states that the whole head is sick (confused, brain washed, unable to reason). Vs 6: Are we rotten? A former salesman that I knew had a saying that the fish rots from the head. Think about that a bit. Vs 7 really makes me believe that Isaiah could be written in current times. Vs 9: Thank God for a small remnant of believers. I don't believe that we are far from the days of Sodom and Gomorrah in our thinking. Vss 11–15 tell us that artificial sacrifices and made up litanies are not what God wants/desires/even demands. Why? Vs 15 tells us that our hands are full of blood. Vss 16–18 tells us to wash, be clean, put away evil, learn to do well, relieve the oppressed, judge the fatherless and to plead for the widows. I love Vs 18: Even though our sins are dark, we can be as pure as snow! What a promise. God really loves us. Vss 20–31: If we refuse to follow God and if we continue to rebel, we will be destroyed.

Chapter 2: Read verse 2. It addresses the last days, telling us that people will flock to Jerusalem and to the mountain of the Lord. Consider the number of people that you know personally that have travelled to Israel in the past few years. Vs 12 through Chapter 4 tells us of the judgment of Judah and Zion.

Chapter 5: Who is my well beloved (Vs 7)?. The Lord of Hosts is my beloved. Vs 1: A vineyard in a very fruitful hill. The Vineyard is the House of Israel. What is the choicest vine? Vs 7 states that Judah is the pleasant plant. That vineyard was his pride and joy. He picked rocks (oh how I hate that job) and fenced it. He also dressed it up with a tower. But alas, Vs 2 tells us that it produced wild grapes. What a disappointment. Think about our disappointment after slaving for a beautiful and productive garden and then think about God's disappointment after putting everything into the Children of Israel and how they rebelled. Today, God must be disappointed because he offers us so much, but we ignore and shun him. Vss 5, 6 tell us that the master of the vineyard destroyed the vineyard. Vs 8: Is this a description of a city? Vs 11: Woe to alcoholics. Vs 14: Hell became larger to hold more people. Are the boundaries being expanded today? Vs 15: A big change. Vss 20–23: Woe. What happened to the evil rulers in Vss 24, 25? Vss 26–30: God will signal to countries far away to come capture the people of Israel until the darkness of sorrow covers the land.

Chapter 6: Vss 1–4: The GLORY of the Lord. What did the Seraphims cry? They were worshipping God. The whole earth is full of God's glory. Isaiah Chapter 6, Verse 5 "Woe is me" cried the prophet after being in the presence of God. Vss 6, 7: Isaiah's lips were cleansed by fire. Vs 8: God called and Isaiah answered. Vss 9, 10: God gave instructions. How long was Isaiah to preach (Vss 11, 12)?

Chapter 7: Vs 14: A prophecy of the virgin birth

Chapter 8: Isaiah was told to fear God and not to join with the other people.

Chapter 9: Compare Vs 2 to Luke 1:79. Vss 6, 7: Prophecy of Jesus.

Chapter 10: Vss 1, 2: False teachers. Read Second Peter chapter 2. Peter taught about false teachers and how to discern between Godly teachers and false teachers. Who said that the Bible is not relevant today? Vs 27: A verse of hope. The yoke is destroyed because of the anointing.

Chapter 11: Vss 1, 2: Prophecies of Jesus. Vss 6–16: A description of when Jesus returns to reign on the earth.

Chapter 12: PRAISE!

Chapter 13: A little geography: Babylon is in Iraq. The Medes and Persians are part of Iran. Vs 1: The burden is the prophecy. Vs 4: This will be directed by the Lord of Hosts. Vs 5: Warriors from everywhere. Vs 10: Darkness. Vs 11: Punishment for evil. Vs 13: There will be a great shaking. Vss 14–18: Total darkness. Vs 19: Babylon was a city of great beauty. The destruction will be like the end of Sodom and Gomorrah. Vss 20–22: Babylon will be inhabited by wild animals. A footnote in my Bible says that Babylon is still desolate. Research on the internet indicates that there are lots of ruins there.

Chapter 14: Vs 7: What a glorious promise. Peace, rest, singing. Is this what we refer to as the end of time or is this when the State of Israel was restored in the Twentieth Century? Vs 12: Isaiah switched gears and talked about Lucifer and his fall from Heaven. Isaiah Chapter 14 verses 13, 14 "For thou hast said in thine heart, I will ascend into heaven, I will exalt my throne above the stars of god: I will sit upon the mount of the congregation, in the sides of the north: I will ascend above the heights of the clouds; I will be like the most High." This was Lucifer's mindset just before he was sent to the pits of hell (Vs 15). Pride goeth before a fall. And his fall was great. Vs 25: Assyria was destroyed (part of Iraq). This includes the city of Nineveh. Remember Jonah? We will study Jonah a bit later, but we are all familiar with his story. Vs 20: The destruction of Palestina (currently Palestine).

Chapter 15: The burden (prophecy) of Moab destroyed. Where is Moab? It is modern day Jordan. They are the descendants of Lot and his daughters. Ancient Sodom and Gomorrah are thought to be in Moab. Ruth was from Moab. She was an ancestor of Jesus.

Chapter 16: The sadness of Moab.

Chapter 17: Prophecy of Damascus (In Syria). It had pitiful harvests.

Chapter 18: More judgments.

Chapter 19: Prophecy of Egypt. Vs 2: Egyptian against Egyptian. Civil war? Brothers against brothers? Vs 3: They sought familiar spirits and wizards (witchcraft). Vss 4–8: The rivers dry up. Vs 16: The people became fearful. Vs 22: God will heal.

Chapter 20: Vss 2, 3: Isaiah was naked and barefoot for three years. Why? Vs 3 tells us it was a sign to Egypt and Ethiopia.

Chapter 21: The prophecy of the desert of the sea and whirlwinds from the desert. Vs 2: A grievous vision for Isaiah. Vs 3: This was as painful to him like pain for a woman in labor. Vs 6: God told Isaiah to set up a watchman. Vss 7–9: The watchman's report. Vs 11: The prophecy of Duma. Vs 13: The prophecy of Arabia.

Chapter 22: Prophecy of the Valley of Vision.

Chapter 23: Prophecy of Tyre.

Chapters 13–23: Prophecies of destruction.

Chapter 24: Description of Desolation.

Chapter 25: PRAISE!

Chapter 26: Isaiah Chapter 26 verse 3 says "Thou will keep him in perfect peace, whose mind is stayed on thee, because he trusteth in Thee". This is one of my favorite verses. This chapter is also a song of salvation. Vss 20 & 21 tell us to enter our chambers and shut the doors until the punishment of the world is done.

Chapter 27: Vs 6 is a prophecy of Israel in our time.

Chapter 28: Definitely addressed those influenced by strong drink which causes error in judgment. Vs 14: The leaders are told to hear the Word. Why do they need to hear and read the Word of the Lord? Vs 15 says it is because they hide behind lies. Don't tell me the Bible is not relevant today.

Chapter 29: Isaiah preached about knowing God. Vss 22–24: There is blessing after discipline.

Chapter 30: Addresses rebellious people. God was gracious. He sent water and light.

Chapter 31: WOE to those who trust in wrong governments and cultures. WOE to them who trust in physical strength instead of God. Vs 6: A Strong warning.

Chapter 32: Vss 15–20: Righteousness rules.

Chapter 33: Vss 15–17 Rewards.

Chapter 34: Isaiah relays the call of God to come near. Vs 7: Did you know that the Bible talks about unicorns? Why does Isaiah say to come near? Read about the judgments written in Chapter 34.

Chapter 35: The wilderness still blossoms. Vss 5, 6: Does Isaiah prophesy about the healing powers of Jesus? Vs 8: The Highway of Holiness.

Chapter 36: The king of Assyria mocked God. Isaiah encouraged Israel to trust in God.

Chapter 37: Hezekiah dressed in sackcloth and sent messengers to Isaiah. Hezekiah compared the troublesome time to a woman in heavy labor. He asked for Isaiah to intercede for them. Vs 7: An interesting way to win the battle. Vss 10–13: More mocking of God. Vs 14: Hezekiah went to the temple to pray. Vss 22–29: God sent a message to Hezekiah through Isaiah. Vss 30–35: God offered proof. Vss 36–38: The king of Assyria was killed by two of his own sons.

Chapter 38: Remember Hezekiah, the King of Judah from Second Kings? He was twenty five when he began to reign according to Second Kings 18:2 and reigned for twenty-nine years in Jerusalem. He did right in the eyes of God. Also, review Second Chronicles chapters 29–32. Vs 1 tells us that Hezekiah was deathly sick. Isaiah came to tell him to put his house in order and prepare to die. What terrible news to deliver. Vs 2: Hezekiah turned his head to the wall and prayed. Vs 4: God sent Isaiah back to Hezekiah to tell him that he would live another fifteen years. Vs 8: God literally turned back the hands of time.

Chapter 39: Vss 4–8: A prophecy that everything in Hezekiah's house would be carried off to Babylon.

Chapter 40: Vs 1: God still commands this today. Vs 3: Read Matthew 3:3. This is another prophecy of Jesus. Vs 8: How long is the Word of our God good? Forever! Vs 11: A prophecy of Jesus. Vs 31: A tremendous promise. I am claiming this during this pandemic. I truly believe it.

Chapter 41: Vs 6: A good verse to live by. Vs 20: Assurance of God's help.

Chapter 42: Vs 1: Does this verse sound familiar? Does this mean that salvation is offered to the Gentiles? Read Luke 3:22. Vss 2, 3: Read Matthew 12:18–21 Vss 10–12: Praise and Glory!

Chapter 43: Vss 1, 2: More wonderful promises. Vss 1–6: Is this a prophecy of the current state of Israel? Vss 18–21: A new thing. God's chosen people.

Chapter 44: Vss 1–4: God loves his people. Vs 8: There are no other Gods. Notice the capital G. There are many gods, but only one God. Vss 9–20: Idolatry is foolishness.

Chapter 45: Cyrus, the king of Persia (Babylon) according to Second Chronicles 36: 22,23. He was told to build a house for God at Jerusalem. Ezra 3:7: Tells us of a grant from Cyrus for the temple. Vss 1–7: Reiteration that God is God. Vs 23: Compare this verse to Philippians 2: 10 & 11. Vs 25: From where comes the justification of Israel? In the Lord.

Chapter 46: Vss 3, 4: God reaffirms that He will deliver Israel. We have seen this within our lifetime as the Country of Israel has been brought back to their homeland and as they have been victorious so many times over much larger countries. Vs 13: Salvation in Zion.

Chapter 47: The humiliation of Babylon. Babylon thought it would be Number one in the world forever. Is It? Vs 13: God mocked the Babylonians by telling them to have the astrologers figure out their next steps.

Chapter 48: Vs 4: Israel is stubborn. Vs 9: Why did God refrain from anger and destruction at that point? Vss 22: No peace for the wicked.

Chapter 49: How many times did God refer to the womb in this chapter? Vss 1, 5, 15: God knows us while we are in the womb. We must break his heart so many times every day with the abortions. How does Psalm 139:14 say that we are made? Remember this when Satan tells you that you are no good. Read this verse from Psalm aloud so he can hear it. CLAIM IT. Vs 1: God calls us from the womb. Today, in 2020, we are told that Abortion Clinics are essential. How can anyone who knows God believe this? It is difficult to read that the king of Egypt called for the destruction of all the Hebrew male babies be killed. We see a correlation to this is Matthew 2:16 when Herod tried to have all the male babies up to two years old killed in Bethlehem. Are the leaders of the world today afraid that a new leader will be born that will usurp their power? Vss 22: Even the Gentiles are offered God's love.

Chapter 50: Are we any different today? Passing the blame? Refusing to take responsibility of our actions? Vs 1: God puts it very plainly. OUR decisions get us into trouble.

Chapter 51: God comforts Zion. Vs 5: His righteousness is near. It is within reach. Vs 8: It is forever.

Chapter 52: Look at the poetry in Vs 7.

Chapter 53: Prophecy of Jesus. Jesus died for us. Repeat: For us.

Chapter 54: Sing praise. Prepare for blessings. Vs 10: His kindness will never leave us. Vs 17: Tells us that there are no weapons effective against God's people. Notice that I use the present tense here.

Chapter 55: Vs 1: A great invitation! To abundant life. Who is the witness in Vs 4? God promises that His Word will not return void. God doesn't speak just to exercise his jaws. Vs 12: A promise of joy and peace. We are told that even the mountains and the trees will make music. Take some time and listen if you do not believe this. Luke 19:40 tells us that if we do not praise, the rocks will cry out.

Chapter 56: More promises of salvation to the Gentiles. This was a big concern for Isaiah. Everyone is offered salvation. What is God's house to be called (Vs 7)?

Chapter 57: We often question why. Vs 1: Why do the righteous perish? They are taken away from the evil to come. Vss 3–11: The ways of the wicked. Vs 12: God is consistent.

Chapter 58: Vs 7: Instructions for holy living. Vss 10–12: The reward of holy living.

Chapter 59: Why do we become separated from God? Is it because God can't reach us? Is it because God can't hear us? Vss 9–14 answers that. Vs 19: For today! The enemy rolls in as a flood but the spirit of the Lord lifts us up. THANK YOU LORD.

Chapter 60: Vs 3: Gentiles shall come to the light. Thank you Lord for the invitation. Vss 6–22: Blessings on Zion from over the known world.

Chapter 61: Vss 1-3: Prophecy of Jesus. Vs 11: Compares the growth of righteousness and praise to the growing of a garden.

Chapter 62: Isaiah talked a lot about the Gentiles and their part in the Kingdom of God. Vs 2: Refers to believers being called Christians first at Antioch. See Acts 11:26 to confirm. This chapter addresses the assurance of salvation.

Chapter 63: Prophecy of Jesus. Vs 3: There would be no one there to stand with Jesus.

Chapter 64: Vss 1–3: Prayer for signs like long ago. Vss 6, 7: Admission of sin.

Chapter 65: God tells the facts. Look at the contrasts in Vss 13–16. Vs 17: A new Heaven and a new earth. Read Revelation 21:1.

Chapter 66: Does Vs 4 sum up the Israelites as well as the people of our time? Isaiah Chapter 66, Verse 22: "For as the new heavens and the new earth, which I will make, shall remain before me, saith the Lord, so shall your seed and your name remain". When is this? Where is this? See Philippians 2:10, 11.

LESSON TWENTY-ONE

JEREMIAH

Jeremiah is known as the weeping prophet. The book of Jeremiah was written between 500 and 600 BC. See Second Kings chapters 22–25. Hilkiah, the high priest, was Jeremiah's father. Jeremiah was written during the reign of kings Josiah, Jehoiakim and Zedekiah. Nebuchadnezar was the king of Babylon. Isaiah warned of coming judgment, but Jeremiah said that the Judgment is here now. Does this sound like our world today? Vs 5 states that God knew Jeremiah even before he was conceived, that he sanctified and ordained him to be a prophet to the nations. Notice that there is an "S" on nations—does this include us? Does this intimate knowledge of Jeremiah before he was conceived apply to us today? Of course. God is the same yesterday, today and forever. Does the acceptance of abortion hurt God? Compare Vss 6–9 to Isaiah 6: 1–10. Also, remember when Moses was called? See Exodus 3: 1– 4:16. Also refer to First Samuel chapter 3.

Chapter 2: Where did Jeremiah get his message (Vs 1)? Who sinned? (Vs 5: the fathers). (Vs 8: the priests, the lawyers, the pastors and the prophets), (Vs 9: The people and their children's children). Vs 28: God mocked the people about their false gods.

Chapter 3: The children of Israel were compared to a harlot—a shameless harlot.

Chapter 4: God called the children to repentance. Vss 20–31 describe desolation.

Chapter 5: Vss 26–31: Does this sound like now?

Chapter 6: Prophecies of the coming destruction.

Chapters 7–15: Jeremiah stood in the gates of the Lord's house to preach. God offered redemption.

Chapter 16: Jeremiah was not allowed to marry or to have children.

Chapter 17: Detailed the sins of Judah.

Chapter 18: God compared the children of Israel to clay in the potter's hands.

Chapters 19–22: More prophecies of doom.

Chapter 23: False teachers and false prophets. Vss 3–6: These are prophecies of Jesus. Vs 21 tells us that not all pastors and teachers are sent from God/that we should always research the scriptures for the truth. Many churches do not even encourage the congregants to bring a Bible to the services. Why?

Chapter 24: God gave an object lesson.

Chapter 25: The seventy years of captivity in Babylon was predicted.

Chapter 26: Vs 8: Jeremiah was threatened. Vs 12: Jeremiah told the people that God gave him the message. Vs 24: Jeremiah was spared.

Chapter 27: God sent the message to be under the yoke of Babylon.

Chapter 28: Hananiah prophesied that the yoke of Babylon would be broken within two years. God told Jeremiah that Hananiah was a false prophet, that the yoke would not be broken in two years. Where in the New Testament do we read about the yoke? See Matthew 11:30 where we are taught that the yoke is easy and the burden is light.

Chapter 29: Jeremiah wrote a letter to the children of Israel telling them to settle in to marry, to have children, to build houses, to plant gardens and to pray for peace while they lived in Babylon. They were to increase Babylon's peace. This sounds like a long term arrangement to me.

Chapter 30: Why was Jeremiah to write in a book? 1). As a permanent record, 2). So everyone could see, 3). To teach that God will bring the children of Israel and Judah back to the land of their fathers. Has this been fulfilled?

Chapter 31: Vs 15 does a beautiful job tying the Old Testament to the New Testament. In Genesis chapter 42 we know that Rachel cried for Joseph when he was gone. Here we read it as a fact. Matthew 2:17–18: Jeremiah is mentioned in the New Testament. Vss 16, 17: Jeremiah spoke of hope. Vss 31–34: A great prophecy. God made a new covenant with Israel that was fulfilled by the death of Jesus on the cross. This is an internal covenant written in our heart—not an external one of laws and sacrifices.

Chapter 32: Jeremiah was in prison. A cousin, Hanameal, went to the prison to sell a field to Jeremiah. With this transaction, Jeremiah knew that restoration would come.

Chapter 33: Jeremiah remained in prison during that time. Vs 3: Often referred to as God's phone number. Jeremiah Chapter 33, verse 3 says "Call unto me, and I will answer thee and shew thee great and mighty things, which thou knowest not". God promised that Zedekiah, the king of Judah, would not die by the sword, but would die peacefully.

Chapter 35: The Rechabites were offered wine, but refused to drink because they had been taught by their fathers not to touch strong drink.

Chapter 36: Baruch became a scribe to write God's messages to Jeremiah because Jeremiah was in prison and could not go around preaching. Baruch read these messages to the people in God's house. Jehudi cut up the book three or four pages at a time and burned them in the fire. Baruch wrote the messages again.

Chapter 37: Jeremiah remained in prison.

Chapter 38: The people did not like God's messages through Jeremiah so they wanted him put to death. He was thrown into a dungeon of mire. Vs 7: Ebedmelech spoke to the king and pleaded for Jeremiah. He was allowed to pull Jeremiah out of the mire. (What a great friend. We need to be pulled out of the mire.) King Zedekiah tried to make a deal with Jeremiah. Jeremiah continued to live in the prison until the time that Jerusalem was taken.

Chapter 39: Nebuchadnezzar, king of Babylon, seized Jerusalem. God had foretold this many times through the messages to Jeremiah. Zedekiah, king of Judah, fled. He was captured by the Chaldeans in the plains of Jericho. Nebuchadnezzar killed the sons of Zedekiah and put out Zedekiah's eyes, bound him in chains and took him to Babylon. The Chaldeans burned the king's house and the people's houses and broke down the walls of Jerusalem. Remember Nehemiah, the builder of the walls? Read Vs 10: The poor were left behind and given vineyards and fields. (An interesting fact.) Vss 11–14: Nebuchadnezzar ordered that Jeremiah be treated well and not to be harmed.

Chapter 40: The captain of the guard offered freedom to Jeremiah. He gave Jeremiah food and a reward. Jeremiah went to live in Mizpah. Mizpah is about five miles Northwest of Jerusalem.

Chapter 41: Fighting and war.

Chapter 42: The remnant asked Jeremiah to pray for them. He prayed and waited on God ten days for a message. He warned them to not to go to Egypt.

Chapter 43: The leaders accused Jeremiah of speaking falsely and they went to Egypt against God's will.

Chapter 44: God laid it on the line. He did not polish his Word or worry about being politically correct. Vs 12: The disobedient would die in Egypt by sword or famine or pestilence. The people thought (Vss 15–19) that the false gods had blessed them with food and wealth. Sound familiar? Are we looking in the wrong places for our needs?

Chapter 45: Vs 5: Do not look for great things to satisfy yourself.

Chapter 46: War on Egypt.

Chapter 47: The Philistines were destroyed.

Chapter 48: Moab was destroyed. Vs 44 is interesting. Fear.

Chapter 49: Judgment on Ammon, Edom and Elam.

Chapters 50-51: The destruction of Babylon. Babylon is modern day Iraq.

Chapter 52: A Repetition of Chapter 39.

LESSON TWENTY-TWO
LAMENTATIONS

Lamentations was written by Jeremiah. This book was read publicly on the anniversary of the destruction of Jerusalem. Remember in First Kings, when Solomon built the temple and the King's House? The beauty was known throughout the world. All of this was destroyed.

Chapter 1: The emptiness of Jerusalem after the fall. Vs 16: Jeremiah wept over Jerusalem.

Chapter 2: More descriptions of desolation.

Chapter 3: Jeremiah's anguish, but read Vss 21–66. Hope. Vs 23: God's faithfulness is great.

Chapter 4: Vs 4: Hunger. There was no bread for the children. Vs 5: The people were so hungry they embraced dung hills. Vs 9: It is better to die by the sword than to die of hunger. Vs 10: They boiled their own children for food.

Chapter 5: A prayer for restoration.

LESSON TWENTY-THREE
EZEKIEL

Ezekiel means God strengthens. This book was written between 500 and 600 BC. It was written by Ezekiel, a priest. He was one of the Jews captured by Nebuchadnezzar. He had visions of God. Read 1:1. As we work through this book, see if you can determine the theme.

Chapter 1: Vs 4: Visions of a whirlwind, a great cloud, fire, a brightness. Vs 5: There were four creatures in the likeness of a man. Vs 6: Each had four faces and four wings. Vs 7: They had straight feet. Vs 8: They had the hands of a man. Vs 9: Their wings were joined together. Read Genesis 3:24 about the cherubims posted at the Garden of Eden. Vs 10: They had the face of a man, the face of a lion, the face of an ox and the face of an eagle. Read Revelations 4:6–8 about the four beasts at the throne. Vs 13: Describes their appearance. Vs 16 talks about a wheel in a wheel. The wheels traveled with the creatures. Vs 26: A great throne like sapphire and a man. Vs 28: The GLORY OF THE LORD. Compare Ezekiel 1:28 (Ezekiel) to Acts 9:4 (Saul) and to Revelation 1:19 (John the Baptist).

Chapter 2: Vs 6: Don't be afraid. Vss 9, 10: A hand came with a book in it. It contained lamentation, mourning and woe.

Chapter 3: Vs 6: God told Ezekiel that the House of Israel would not listen. Compare Vss 12–14 to Acts Chapter 2. Vs 26: Moses thought that his tongue would stick to his mouth. Compare Moses's calling in Exodus 3 to Ezekiel's calling. Vs 27: See God's message to the Church of Ephesus in The Revelation 2:7, to the Church of Smyrna in The Revelation 2:11, to the Church of Pergamos in The Revelation 2:17 and to the Church of Thyatira in The Revelation 2:29.

Chapters 4–6: Prophecies of judgment against Jerusalem. 5:10: They will resort to cannibalism to survive. 5:12: One third would die from pestilence and famine, one third by the sword, and one third would be captured to become slaves. In Chapter 6, God promised to destroy the groves and the high places of idol worship. In chapter 6: Vss 7, 10, 13, 14 we see the theme of the book four times.

Chapter 7: Vss 4, 9, 27: This statement appears three more times. Vs 25: Destruction will come and they will seek peace, but there won't be any peace. NOTE: Does God have a message for us today?

WHY DOES GOD PRONOUNCE JUDGMENT?

Chapters 8, 9. 8:6–16: A list of abominations that God showed Ezekiel. In 9:4, the scribe was told to put a mark on the foreheads of those who were sorry for evil. (THIS IS DIFFERENT THAN THE MARK OF THE BEAST.) In 9:6, they were told to not disturb anyone with this mark.

Chapter 10: More descriptions of the cherubims and the wheel from Chapter 1.

Chapter 11: God took Ezekiel to see the leaders and rulers who devised evil. God gave him a message for the powerful evil men in Vs 10. Vs 12 repeats this.

Chapter 12: Vss 16, 20, 25: The theme repeats three times in this chapter.

Chapter 13: Foolish prophets. Vss 14, 21: Two more repetitions of the theme.

Chapter 14: A problem of idols. Vs 13: God promised famine if the evil continued. Vs 8: The theme again.

Chapter 15: Vs 7: The theme again.

Chapter 16: God loved Jerusalem. He had taken care of Jerusalem. Look how she was dressed and how well she had been fed. Vss 15–19: Jerusalem did not follow God, but instead chose to play the harlot. Vs 20: Not only did the people defy God, the next generation was dedicated to evil. The people of Jerusalem were for sale to any nation. Vs 38: God shall judge. Vs 44: As the mother, so the daughter. The apple doesn't fall far from the tree. Vs 63: The theme again.

Chapter 17: God gave a riddle to Ezekiel about a great eagle with great wings. Is this a reference to the children of Israel being carried away into captivity?

Chapter 18: Each person is judged on their own merit. Vs 4: The person who sins will die. Vss 5–9: He that does no evil will live. Vss 10–13: If a son sins, the son will die. Vss 14–17: What about a son and the sin in his father? Vs 20: The son is not responsible for his father's sins. The father is not responsible for the sins of the son. Vs 21: A great promise. If you do no evil and follow God, you shall live. Vs 32: God has no pleasure in the death of one who does evil. Turn to the Lord and Live.

Chapter 19: See Genesis 49:9: Judah is known as a lion's whelp.

Chapter 20: Vs 12: The theme again. God continued to plead with the children of Israel. Vss 33–38: God promised to bring them back from the scattered places. Vs 42 & 44: The theme again.

Chapter 21: Vs 28: The Ammonites would be no more.

Chapter 22: God pointed out certain sins of the people. Vs 16: The theme again. Vs 30: God was looking for a man to stand in the gap but He did not find any. Would He find any today?

Chapter 23: God compared Samaria and Jerusalem to two harlots.

Chapter 24: The parable of the cooking pot. Vss 15–18: Ezekiel's wife died. Vs 27: Did you find the theme of the book again?

Chapter 25: Vss 5, 17: The theme again. The end of the Ammonites. Vs 10: Tells us that the Ammonites will not even be remembered.

Chapter 26: The destruction of Tyrus.

Chapter 27: God told Ezekiel to lament to Tyrus. He recited the trade practices of that seaport city.

Chapter 28: God had a message for the prince of Tyrus. His wisdom made him proud. Ezekiel was told to lament to king of Tyrus. Vs 23, 24, 26: The theme three more times.

Chapter 29: Vs 5: The Egyptians were given to the beasts to eat. Vss 6, 9, 16, 21: The theme continues. Vs 9: Prophesy that Egypt would be desolate and waste land. Vss 9–15: The desolation of Egypt. Vs 21: The horn (power) of the house of Israel.

Chapter 30: More details of the fall of Egypt. Vss 8, 19, 25, 26: The theme four more times.

Chapter 31: Vs 4: Irrigation? More details of the destruction of Pharaoh and Egypt.

Chapter 32: Vs 15: The theme again. A lament over Pharaoh and Egypt.

Chapter 33: Setting up a watchman. Vs 3: The watchman was to blow the trumpet. As you read this chapter, determine the responsibility of the watchmen and the responsibility of those that heard the trumpet. Was Ezekiel the watchman? Vss 25–26: If the people of Israel are wicked, should they inherit the land? Vs 29: Are you keeping count of the theme?

Chapter 34: Is God referring to preachers and teachers when he talks about shepherds not feeding their flock? Vs 5: The people (sheep) were scattered because there was no shepherd. Vs 11: A great promise! God will search for the lost sheep! Read Matthew 18:11–13. Vs 13: God will bring the sheep home and feed them in Israel. Ezekiel Chapter 34, Verse 15: "I will feed my flock, and I will cause them to lie down, saith the Lord God". Do sheep lie down when they are troubled or hungry or agitated? Do we rest calmly when we are upset? Is this chapter a prophecy of Jesus?

Chapter 35: Why would God make Mt Seir desolate? Vs 5: Because of hatred toward the children of Israel. Vss 9, 12, 15: The theme three more times.

Chapter 36: Blessings in Israel. Vss 11, 23, 38: The theme repeats. Why did God bless Israel? Vs 22: For His sake. Vss 24, 25: He will clean them up. Vs 26: God will give them a new heart and a new spirit. Vss 27–38: Continued blessings.

Chapter 37: Dry bones! The valley was full of dry bones. God told Ezekiel to preach to the dry bones and tell them to hear the Word of God. How many people would follow God's instructions and do this today? We would get carted off to the mental ward. Let us follow the progress of this preaching. Vs 5: God breathed into them (the dry bones). Vs 6: Sinews and flesh. What happened? Vs 7: A noise, a shaking as the bones came together. Then there was skin. Vs 9: The 4 winds breathed on them. What is this about? The bones were the house of Israel without hope. Vs 12: God promised to open the graves. See Vss 13, 28 for the theme. Vs 14: The House of Israel will be restored to their own land. Vs 16: Write "For Judah" on one stick and write "For Joseph" on another stick. Vs 17: Join the sticks together and they shall become one. Vss 19–27: Israel is to be united and a peace covenant will be made. Why?

Chapter 38: Gog and its allies will war against Israel when they are home. Recognize any of these places? Magog is the Southern Soviet Union; Persia is Iran; Ethiopia is East Africa; Libya is in Northern Arabia; Tarshish is Southern Spain. This chapter talks about the latter days. Is this prophecy of the end of time? Vs 19: A great shaking in Israel. Vs 21: Brother shall stand against brother. Vs 22: God will send fire, brimstone and hail. Why? Vs 23: God will be known and magnified in the eyes of many nations.

Chapter 39: God will destroy five-sixths of the people and give them to the beasts of the field. Vss 6, 7, 22: The theme again. Vss 25–29: God will bless the nation of Israel.

Chapter 40: Is this a vision? A very precise measurement of the temple. Also, this chapter describes the furnishing of the temple.

Chapters 41 & 42: More dimensions of the temple which includes accommodations for the priests.

Chapter 43: Altars and sacrifices.

Chapter 44: There were some people not allowed to enter the temple. Some were not allowed to be priests. Vs 15: The sons of Zadok who remained obedient would minister to the Lord. Vss 16–31: Rules for the priests.

Chapter 45: Dividing the land. A portion is set aside for God's use and for sacrifices and offerings. Vs 19: Blood applied to the door posts. Vs 21: Passover.

Chapter 46: The gate of the inner court opens only on the Sabbath and on the days of the New Moon. A description of how worship was to be done. Vs 9: Don't exit the gate that you entered. Vs 13: A young lamb was to be sacrificed every morning.

Chapter 47: Water flowing from under the door eastward. How deep was the water? At 1000 cubits (1500 feet) out from the door, it was up to the ankles. At 3000 feet, it was up to his knees. At 4500 feet out it was up to the loins. At 6000 feet out, it was a river that could not be forded. Vss 13–23: boundaries and borders.

Chapter 48: How the land was to be divided.

LESSON TWENTY-FOUR
DANIEL

Written by Daniel between 500 and 600 BC.

Daniel means God is Judge. Daniel was a captive of Nebuchadnezzar in Babylon. Daniel 6:3 tells us that Daniel had an excellent spirit. Daniel was recognized in Matthew 24:15 by Jesus as a prophet.

Chapter 1: Daniel was without blemish, well-favored, skillful in all wisdom, cunning in knowledge and he understood science according to verse 4. Verse 5: Daniel was to be nourished with the king's food and wine in preparation for serving the king. Vs 7: Daniel was renamed Belteshazzar, Shadrach was renamed Hananiah, Meshach was renamed Michael, Abednego was renamed Azariah. Vs 8: Daniel refused the king's meat. Vs 12: He asked permission to eat only vegetables and to drink water for ten days to prove that he was healthy. Vs 15: After ten days, the Hebrew men appeared healthier than those eating the king's meat. Vs 16: So they were allowed to continue the vegetables and water. Vs 20: The four Hebrew men were ten times smarter, healthier, and wiser than the court magicians and astrologers.

Chapter 2: Nebuchadnezzar had a dream. Who did he call? The magicians, the astrologers, the sorcerers and the Chaldeans. See Genesis 41:8. Who did Pharaoh call to interpret his dreams? The magicians, the wise men. Who do we call today when we are troubled? Doctors. Who helped Nebuchadnezzar? Daniel through God. Who will help us? GOD. Vss 12–18: Daniel and his three friends were considered wise men and would have been slain but Daniel called on God for wisdom. Vss 19–23: Daniel blessed God. Vss 28, 29: Daniel gave God credit for everything. Vss 31–49: Daniel explained Nebuchadnezzar's dream. The head was of gold, the breastplate of silver, the belly and thighs were brass, the legs were of iron and the feet were made of iron and clay. A stone, not made with hands, broke the feet of iron and clay. The entire image was broken to bits and the wind carried them away. The stone became a great mountain. Vss 39–43: Another ruler would arise, inferior to Nebuchadnezzar, then another kingdom and a fouth kingdom. The fourth kingdom would be partly strong and partly broken but not united. Vss 44, 45: Then! A kingdom that was never to be destroyed and was to consume all the other kingdoms. Vss 46–49: Nebuchadnezzar worshipped Daniel and made him a ruler. See Genesis 41:41: Joseph became a ruler. He also interpreted dreams.

Chapter 3: Nebuchadnezzar made a golden image ninety feet tall and nine feet wide. Vss 2, 3: All rulers were invited to the dedication. Vss 4–7: Everyone was ordered to bow and worship the image. Vss 8–12: Chaldeans reported to Nebuchadnezzar that certain Jews were not worshipping the image. Vs 13: Meshach Shadrach and Abednego were brought to Nebuchadnezzar. Vss 19–21: Nebuchadnezzar ordered the furnace to be fired seven times hotter and ordered his soldiers to bind them and to throw them into the fire. Vss 22: The fire was so hot that it burned the soldiers to death. Vss 23: The three Jews fell into the furnace. Vs 25: Nebuchadnezzar saw four men in the fire. They were unhurt. He recognized that one was "like the Son of God" according to Daniel Chapter 3, Verse 25. Vs 26: Nebuchadnezzar called them out of the fire. Vs 27: The rulers saw that they were not hurt. There wasn't even the smell of fire or smoke on them. Vss 28–30: Nebuchadnezzar ordered a protection decree over the three Hebrew children.

Chapter 4: Nebuchadnezzar dreamed of a tree in the middle of the earth that reached unto heaven and it spread shade and produced lots of fruit. Someone came from heaven and said to cut down the tree and to shake down the fruit. However, the stump was to be left intact. Vs 16: The heart of a beast was to be given up to the stump. Why? Read Vs 17. Daniel interpreted. The tree represented Nebuchadnezzar over his kingdom. Daniel told Nebuchadnezzar that he would be driven out to live with beasts of the field and would eat grass. The stump represented that his kingdom would remain secure until Nebuchadnezzar realized that the Most High reigns. Vs 33: Nebuchadnezzar's hair became like eagle feathers and his nails like bird claws. Vss 34–37: After this dream, Nebuchadnezzar praised God. What is the theme of Chapter 4? According to Daniel, Chapter 4, Verses 17, 25, and 32 "the most High ruleth in the kingdom of men, and giveth it to whomsoever he will".

Chapter 5: Here comes another king—Belshazzar. Vss 2 and 13 tell us that he was the son of Nebuchadnezzar. Vs 4: He worshipped idols. Vs 5: Fingers of a man's hand appeared and wrote on the wall. Vs 6: A lot of shaking was going on. Belshazzar's knees knocked. Vs 7: Here again, the astrologers, the Chaldeans, and the soothsayers were called for interpretation. Vs 8: They could not interpret it. Vs 10: The queen advised Belshazzar to call on Daniel. Vs 16: The king offered gifts to Daniel. Vs 17: Daniel refused the gifts. Vss 18-23: Daniel reviewed Nebuchadnezzar's life and compared it to Belshazzar's life. Vss 36–28: Interpretation—the end of the kingdom. Vs 30: Fulfillment—Belshazzar was slain that night. Vs 31: Darius took the kingdom.

Chapter 6: Another king replaced Nebuchadnezzar. There was jealousy in the kingdom. Some of the rulers petitioned the king to attempt to trap Daniel. Vs 10: Daniel prayed in front of his window three times every day even after the decree was signed. A bunch of tattletales went to king Darius with their report that Daniel was praying to God. Vs 16: Darius knew that God would deliver Daniel. Vs 17: The lions' den was sealed with a stone. Compare to Matthew 27:57–66. Vs 18: Darius fasted that night. He could not sleep. He went to the den early the next morning to check on Daniel. Vs 22: Daniel gave God the credit for his safety. Why wasn't Daniel harmed? Read V 23. Vs 24: A reversal!

The accusers and their families were cast in the lions' den and the lions destroyed them immediately. Vss 26, 27: Darius declared God to the people.

Chapter 7: It appears that this chapter is out of sequence. This time Daniel had a dream. Vs 3: Four beasts came up out of the sea. Read Revelation 13:1. It tells us of a beast rising out of the sea with seven heads and ten horns. There were crowns on the horns. Blasphemy was on its head. Vs 4: The first beast was like a lion with eagle's wings but it stood up like a man. Vs 5: The second beast was like a bear with three ribs in its mouth. Vs 6: The third beast was like a leopard with four wings. It had four heads. Vs 7: The fourth beast was dreadful and strong with iron teeth and ten horns. Vs 8: Three horns were plucked out and a smaller horn grew with eyes in the horn like the eyes of a man. This new horn also had a mouth to speak. Vs 9: The Ancient of Days sat and a fiery stream came from him. MILLIONS ministered to him and the books were opened. God's judgment day? Vs 11: The beast was slain and given to the flame. Is this Satan being cast into hell? Remember that this book was written about 500 years before the birth of Christ, but Daniel appears to be talking about the great judgment day. Vs 12: The other beasts lost their dominion but they lived a while longer. Vs 13: Does Daniel foresee Jesus? The Son of Man? Vs 14: The Son of Man was given dominion and glory and the kingdom—an everlasting dominion which won't be destroyed! Now, Daniel needed help with interpretation. Vs 17: The beasts are four kings. Vs18: The saints shall take the kingdom forever. FOREVER! Vs 19: The fourth beast with ten horns had a small horn that warred against the saints (Vs 23). There will be a kingdom, different from all the others. Each horn represents a king that arises and falls. Vs 25: Is Daniel predicting current times? The king speaks against the Most High and wears out the saints, and wants to change everything. Vs 27: VICTORY! The saints prevail.

Chapter 8: Vs 2: Daniel had another vision. This was about a ram with two horns. Now this is not unusual, but one horn was taller than the other. The Ram pushed North, South and West. No beasts could stand up to him. A he goat came from the West without touching the ground. This goat had a horn between his eyes and he charged the ram. The he goat was angry at the ram and hit him, breaking off the two horns of the ram. The ram became powerless and the he goat stomped the ram. Vs 8: The he goat became great and strong. The great horn broke off and four new horns appeared. Vs 9: A little horn grew out of one of his new horns. This newest horn became great. Vs 10: This newest horn cast down some of the hosts of heaven and some of the stars. Vs 14: The transgression of desolation was to last 2300 days before the sanctuary would be cleansed. Vs 16: A man's voice told the angel Gabriel to make Daniel understand the vision. Daniel was afraid. Did Gabriel tell Daniel that this is a vision of the end of time? Vs 18: Daniel was in a deep sleep but Gabriel sat him up. Explanation: The ram with two horns are the kings of Media and Persia. The he goat is the king of Greece. The great horn on the he goat is the one king. The four replacement horns are the four kingdoms. Vs 23: A king with a fierce countenance stands up. Vs 24: This king will be powerful (not of his own power). By what power? He will prosper and destroy the mighty and holy people. Vs 25: This king will stand against the Prince of princes (the Lord) and the king shall be broken!.

Chapter 9: Daniel sought the Lord with fasting, sackcloth and ashes. Vss 4–19: Daniel's prayer of Confession, Acknowledging the Power of God, Admission of confusion, Acknowledging that God allowed this to turn the people back to God, Beseeching God to hear the supplication, Asking for forgiveness. Vs 22: Gabriel came to tell Daniel that his is loved. Vss 25–27: God set a timeline.

Chapter 10: Vs 2: Daniel mourned three weeks. He ate no sweets and drank no wine. Vs 5: A man dressed in linen. Read Vs 6, then read Revelation 1:13–20. Vss 11–21: Is this the angel Gabriel addressing Daniel? Was the angel Michael assigned to Daniel?

Chapter 11: I see this as an explanation of the earlier chapters.

Chapter 12: Is this about the end of time? Vs 1: There is trouble like never before. Is YOUR name written in the Book? Vs 2: Those in the graves shall awake. Some to everlasting life and some to everlasting contempt. Daniel Chapter 12, Verse 4: "But thou, O Daniel, shut up the words, and seal the book, even to the time of the end: many shall run to and fro, and knowledge shall be increased". Read Second Timothy 3:7. Does this sound familiar? When will the Book be unsealed? Revelation 22:10.

Read Mark 13:4. Peter, James, John and Andrew asked a question in the New Testament. Read Mark 13:5–20. The last couple of verses of the Book of Daniel give us a number of days. But remember, only God knows the times. Rev 22:7, Rev 22:12, Rev 22:20 WARNING. Do not be deceived. Rev 22: 18–19: If we add or subtract from God's Word, we will have plagues and our name will be taken out of the Book of Life.

LESSON TWENTY-FIVE
HOSEA

Written during the time of Isaiah. Hosea means deliverer. A very unusual book.

Chapter 1: Vs 2: God told Hosea to marry a prostitute. Vs 8: Was this child Hosea's son? Read Vs 9 and decide. Maybe he wasn't.

Chapter 2: Hosea asked the children to plead with their mother to quit being a prostitute. Is this a correlation of God pleading with His children to quit chasing false gods? Read Chapter 1: Vss 2–23.

Chapter 3: Vs 2: Hosea bought Gomer, his wife, for fifteen pieces of silver.

Chapter 4: Why is it important to study God's Word? Read Vs 6. It tells us that people are destroyed for lack of knowledge.

Chapter 5: How sad! Read Vs 6. Vs 8: Blow the trumpet. Sound an alarm. Vs 15: God will hide His face until the people seek Him.

Chapter 6: Vs 3: If we recognize the Lord, He will come like rain.

Chapter 7: The adulterers are compared to a baker whose heart is like an oven.

Chapter 8: Sound the trumpet. Vs 7: Sow the wind. Reap the whirlwind. Vs 13: God did not accept their sacrifices.

Chapter 9: The judgment of Israel.

Chapter 10: Vs 10: Israel was an empty vine. Israel continued to sin.

Chapter 11: God tells of His love for Israel by getting them out of Egypt. Even though Israel worshipped other gods, God would restore them.

Chapter 12: God dealt with Jacob even though he came out of the womb holding Esau's heel. Read Genesis 25:26.

Chapter 13: God continued to ache for Israel.

Chapter14: God describes redemption.

LESSON TWENTY-SIX
JOEL

Chapter 1: Locusts, cankerworms and caterpillars destroyed the crops. Read Revelation 9:7 about the locusts. Vs 13: Ministers were to fast and pray all night in sackcloth. Then they were to call a national fast. Vss 17–20: Even the animals were hungry and thirsty.

Chapter 2: Joel was told to blow the trumpet and to sound the alarm. We read this warning in Hosea also. Joel describes the Day of the Lord—panic, darkness, earthquakes, while the sun, the moon and the stars won't shine. Vss 12, 13: God offered deliverance. Vs 15: Blow the trumpet! Vs 21: **HOPE**. The Lord will do great things. Vss 23–32: God promised plenty. Read Isaiah 2:4 and compare to Joel 3:9, 10. We need to BLOW THE TRUMPET and SOUND THE ALARM today in America.

LESSON TWENTY-SEVEN
AMOS

This book was written by Amos during the reign of Uzziah. See Isaiah 6:1.

Chapter 1: Vss 3–5: Damascus destroyed by fire. Vss 6–8: Gaza destroyed by fire. Vss 9, 10: Tyrus destroyed by fire. Vss 11, 12: Edom destroyed by fire. Vss 13–15: Ammon destroyed by fire. Amos Chapter 1: Verses 3, 6, 9, 11, 13 "Thus saith the Lord".

Chapter 2: Vss 1–3 Moab destroyed by fire. Vss 4, 5: Judah destroyed by fire. Vs 6: Israel destroyed by fire. Amos described the sins of Israel. God reminded the Israelites of their deliverance from Israel. Amos Chapter 2, Verses 1, 4, 6 "Thus saith the Lord".

Chapter 3: Vs 11: Amos exhorted the people to hear the Word of the Lord. Vss 3–8: Questions to consider. This was written to Israel and to Judah. Amos Chapter 3, Verses 11, 12 "Thus saith the Lord". Vs 12: Just like a shepherd that was too late that he was only able to retrieve parts of a lamb, so it will be with the Israelites in Samaria when they are rescued.

Chapter 4: Where is Bashon? It is east of the Jordan River. Is God calling the women fat cows? (kine is cow). They will be led away by hooks in their noses. I like this chapter in The Living Bible. If you have access to one, read it. Vss 4, 5: God mocked their offerings and sacrifices. Vss 6–11: A listing of judgments on the people. Vs 13: God identified Himself.

Chapter 5: Vss 4, 6: The people are told to seek God so they will live. Vss 18–20: A description of the Day of the Lord. Vss 21–27: God doesn't sugar coat. He despised (and continues to despise) hypocrisy and fake worship.

Chapter 6: WOE. Vss 1–6: Woe to those who ignore world happenings. Woe to those who only care for themselves and are not concerned about others. Woe to them that refuse to believe that punishment is coming.

Chapter 7: Vs 1: A swarm of locusts that ate everything in sight. Vs 2: Amos pleaded with God to hold the plague of locusts from the second harvest. Vs 3: God held the plague. James Chapter 5, verse 16: "The effectual fervent prayer of a righteous man availeth much". Do you believe that prayer changes things? Would God consider you an effectual fervent prayer warrior? Vss 7, 8: God set a plumbline. Why do we use plumblines today? Vss 10–13: False leaders. Amaziah the priest accused Amos of being a traitor and tried to run him out of the country. Vss 14–17: Amos told Amaziah that God had called him to prophesy.

Chapter 8: A vision of a basket of ripe fruit to represent the Children of Israel being ripe for punishment. Vs 3: There was howling in the temple and dead bodies everywhere. Vss 4–6: Cheating the poor. Using false scales. Trying to get rid of the poor and buying the poor to become slaves. Vs 8: The earth will tremble, everyone will mourn, there will be floods. Vs 9: The sun will set at noon. The earth will be dark during the day. Vss 10–14: Feasts turn into mourning. Songs become laments. People will wear sackcloth. People will become bald. A famine of hearing from God so prevalent that people will wander the earth in search of God. Young people shall faint. We need to GET READY.

Chapter 9: Vss 1–4: God will shake the temple. ALL will be killed by the falling temple. No one can hide from God – even in hell or at the bottom of the deepest sea. Vs 8: God will scatter the Children of Israel all over the world. We know that this happened. Vs 11: The City of David will return to its former glory. Vs 12: Israel will possess Edom. Vs 13: There will be an abundance of crops. Vs 14: Fortunes will be restored. Vs 15: Once Israel is restored, it won't be pulled up again! Reread Vs 15. Israel has been restored today and Israel WILL NOT BE PULLED UP AGAIN!

LESSON TWENTY-EIGHT
OBADIAH

I don't know the time frame of this book. Vs 1: A vision about Edom. The Edomites were descendants of Esau. Remember in Genesis chapter 25 that Esau was the oldest twin. Genesis 25:28–34: Esau sold his birthright to Jacob for food. Genesis chapter 27 tells us that Rebekah and Jacob tricked him out of his blessing from Isaac. Genesis 28:9: Esau married into Ishmael's family. Genesis 32:11: Jacob asked God to protect him from Esau. This entire book (only has 1 chapter) is about the vision of the destruction of Edom. Vs 7: Edom's allies turned against them. Vss 10, 11: Why were Edom's sins exposed? Because Edom deserted Israel in Israel's time of need. Vs 17: Prophecy: Israel will occupy their homeland. FULFILLED.

LESSON TWENTY-NINE
JONAH

We are all familiar with the story of Jonah.

Chapter 1: Vss 1–3: God told Jonah to go to Nineveh to tell the people that God was going to destroy them. Jonah was afraid. Instead of heading to Nineveh, he boarded a ship bound for Joppa. He hid in the dark hold of the ship. Vss 4, 5: A great storm hit the ship. Vs 7: Jonah drew the short straw which determined Jonah to be the reason of the storm. Vss 9, 10: Jonah admitted that he was running from God. Vs 12: He offered to be thrown into the sea. Vs 15: When Jonah hit the sea, the storm stopped. Vs 17: Jonah caught a new ride—inside a great fish for three days and nights.

Chapter 2: Jonah prayed inside that big fish. Vs 9: Jonah promised to worship only God from that point.

Chapter 3: Jonah went to Nineveh after taking that detour. As Jonah preached, the people repented and put on sackcloth. The king declared a fast—even from water. He told everyone to cry out to God and to turn away from evil. Vs 16: God halted His plan to destroy Nineveh.

Chapter 4: Jonah was angry that God saved Nineveh and he wanted to die (see Vs 3). Refer to First Kings 19:4. Elijah wanted to die. God had a lesson for Jonah Vss 4–11.

LESSON THIRTY
MICAH

Chapter 1: God gave messages to Micah. Micah prophesied during the reign of Jotham, Ahab and Hezekiah. Vs 5: Why? Because of the sins of Israel and Judah. God even pointed out the sins: oppression and Idolatry. Vss 6, 7: Samaria would be destroyed. Vs 16: The children were taken as slaves.

Chapter 2: Woe to schemers. Vss 3, 5: God gave the warning. Vs 6: The people refused to listen. Vss 8, 9: The shirts were stolen off the backs of the people and the widows lost their homes. Vss 12, 13: Prophecy of Israel's restoration.

Chapter 3: Listen up leaders! You, as a leader, should know right from wrong. Yet, you hate good and cling to the evil. Vs 4: You plead for help after you are so evil? Vs 5: False prophets lead people astray. Vs 8: Micah was filled with power. He became fearless to announce God's judgment. Vs 12: Why would Jerusalem be destroyed? Because of corrupt leaders and false prophets.

Chapter 4: Vs 2: The Lord shall rule from Jerusalem. Read Isaiah 2: Vss 2, 3. Compare Joel 3:10, Isaiah 2:4, and Micah 4:3. Vss 4–8 talk about a glorious time.

Chapter 5: Vss 2–4: Bethlehem would produce a ruler of Israel. See Matthew 2:6 and Luke 2: Vss 4–7. Vs 8: The strength of Israel. Remember the six day war in 1967? June 5-10, 1967. Who won? Tiny Israel won the Gaza Strip and the Sinai Peninsula from Egypt; they won the West Bank including East Jerusalem from Jordan and they won the Golan Heights from Syria.

Chapter 6: God told his people to stand up and to state their complaint against Him. Vss 2–5: God voiced His complaint. Read Vs 8. What did God require of them and still require of us? Vs 14: The people will eat and never have enough, they will try to save money but it will be taken away. Vs 15: They will plant crops they won't harvest.

Chapter 7: Vss 1–4: Evil runs rampant. Vss 5, 6: Don't trust anyone. Vss 11, 12: Cities will be rebuilt and be prosperous. They will be honored by many people. Vs 13: But first, destruction would come because of wickedness. Vss 18–20: There is no other God like our God. He loves us. He is merciful.

LESSON THIRTY-ONE
NAHUM

This was written years after Jonah's missionary trip. Remember that the people repented after Jonah preached. Nineveh is an Assyrian city in upper Mesopotamia (modern day Iraq) and is located on the Tigris River. In 612 BC, it was destroyed by the Medes and Babylonians. We first read about Nineveh in Genesis Chapter 10.

Chapter 1: Vs 1: The prophecy about Nineveh. Vs 3: The Lord is slow to anger, the Lord is powerful. Vs 6: God's anger is fierce. Vs 9: What could Nineveh imagine against God? One hit is all it would take.

Chapter 2: Vss 3-6: Description of the battle. Vs 7: The Queen was led away captive and Nineveh was destroyed.

Chpater 3: Woe to Nineveh. Why? Because Nineveh sold her soul to false gods and to witchcraft.

LESSON THIRTY-TWO

HABAKKUK

Chapter 1: Habakkuk was a minor prophet. Vss 2–4: This sounds like America today. The Living Bible says in Habakkuk Chapter 1, verses 3, 4 "Wherever I look there is oppression and bribery and men who love to argue and to fight. The law is not enforced and there is no justice given in the courts, for the wicked far outnumber the righteous and bribes and trickery prevail." Vss 5–11: God sent the fierce Chaldeans to destroy the land.

Chapter 2: Vss 2, 3: God told Habakkuk that things would happen slowly. Vs 13: Godless gains turn to ashes. Vs 14: What a glorious promise! Vs 20: A chant that some denominations use today to open their Sunday service.

Chapter 3: Vs 2: Habakkuk's prayer. Vss 3–19: A wonderful Hymn of Praise!

LESSON THIRTY-THREE
ZEPHANIAH

Written during the time of Josiah, king of Judah.

Chapter 1: Vss 2–18: Prophecy of a great destruction.

Chapter 2: Zephaniah exhorted the people to pray and to walk humbly. All the cities around would be destroyed but see Vs 7. The remnant of Judah would be restored. Vss 12–14: The beasts would inhabit the old Nineveh.

Chapter 3: The wickedness of Jerusalem. Vss 14–20: God told the people to praise Him. At last their troubles would be over. Vs 20: God will bring the people home and restore their fortunes. Think about modern-day Israel.

LESSON THIRTY-FOUR
MATTHEW

WELCOME to the New Testament studies—the fulfillment of the Old Testament. There are four Gospels named after their authors: Matthew (Levi), Mark (John Mark), Luke (the physician), John (The Beloved, Son of Thunder). Matthew was a publican—a hated tax collector who became one of the twelve disciples.

Chapter 1: Gives us the forty-two generations from Abraham to Joseph. Luke 3: 23–38 takes that genealogy back to Adam. However, Jesus was born of a virgin after being conceived of the Holy Spirit. So on His father's side, the true genealogy was very simple: The Holy Ghost, Jesus. We do not learn any of His mother's history, except that she was a young virgin, until we begin to study Luke. 1:18 begins the fulfillment of prophesy beginning at Genesis 3:15 when God promised a Deliverer to conquer Satan. 1:18–25: Mary and Joseph were engaged. Mary was a virgin when she was found to be pregnant by the Holy Ghost. Matthew tells us that an angel visited Joseph with the news that Mary was pregnant by the Holy Ghost (Vs 20). The angel even told Joseph that the Baby would be named Jesus. Vs 22 gives the first New Testament reference to fulfillment. Vs 25: Mary and Joseph remained chaste until after the birth of Jesus.

Chapter 2: Vs 1: Jesus was born in Bethlehem of Judea as prophesied by Micah in Micah 5:2. Wise men from the East were looking for the King of the Jews. They were astrologers following a star to find him. They went to Jerusalem and questioned Herod the king as to where the baby was so they could worship Him. They were classified as wise men but did not know that they were actually seeking THE SAVIOUR. Herod was scared and called a meeting with the priests and scribes who told him that the Old Testament prophecies indicated that a Saviour (Deliverer, Governor) would be born to the house of David. Herod sent the wise men to Bethlehem with instructions to return to Jerusalem and tell him where the child was. Vss 9, 10: They followed the star to Jesus. They fell down and worshipped. Philippians 2:10 tells us that every knee shall bow at the name of Jesus. This was the beginning of true worship. Vs 12: God warned the wise men in a dream not to return to King

Herod. They obeyed. Vss 13–15: God told Joseph in a dream to take Mary and Jesus to Egypt until further notice. He did. Vs 16: Herod was mad and had all the children two years old and younger in and around Bethlehem killed in an attempt to destroy Jesus. Jeremiah 31:15 predicted the murder of these babies. Vss 19, 20: God told Joseph in another dream to take his family to Israel. Vs 22: Instead, he was afraid and took them to Nazareth (his hometown).

Chapter 3: This chapter introduces us to John the Baptist. He is not the John who wrote the Book of John and Revelations. John the Baptist was actually a cousin of Jesus's mother Mary as we read in Luke Chapter 1. John the Baptist preached for the people to repent and to get ready for Jesus. We see John the Baptist as a mountain man dressed in camel hair and eating locusts and wild honey. Vss 5, 6: He baptized those who confessed. Vss 7–10: John the Baptist chastised the Pharisees and the Sadducees because he discerned that they were not truly repentant. Vs 11: John told the people that he wasn't worthy to even carry the shoes of Jesus. Vss 13–17: Jesus asked John to baptize him. He did. The affirmation came when the heavens opened and the Spirit of God descended like a dove upon Jesus and a voice from heaven announced that Jesus was truly the Son of God!

Chapter 4: Jesus went into the wilderness and fasted forty days and nights. Vss 3–10 tell us that Satan tried to tempt Jesus. Jesus answered with scripture each time and defeated Satan. Vss 13–17: Jesus began His ministry in Capernaum. Vss 18–22: Jesus called two sets of brothers as His disciples (Peter, Andrew, James, John). All four were fishermen. They immediately followed Jesus. Vss 23–25: Jesus continued preaching throughout Galilee (currently Northern Israel), healing and being followed by multitudes.

Chapters 5–7: The Sermon on the Mount by Jesus. 5:3–12 contains the Beatitudes. Read 5:18. Jesus clearly states that not even a mark is to be removed from the law until everything is fulfilled. What does this say about people who pick and choose which parts of the bible are pertinent or true? 5:22 cross-referenced to First John 3:15 says that hating anyone is the same as murder. 5:27 broadens the definition of adultery to include our thoughts. 5:48 is the command from Jesus to be perfect. In chapter 6:1–8 Jesus tells us not to do good just to be noticed. 6:9–13 is the model prayer taught by Jesus. 6:16–18: Another teaching to avoid piety and the praise of people. Do you agree with 6:21? Was Jesus familiar with the Old Testament? Read 6:29 and 7:1. 7:15–24 contain warnings for all times. Be careful. Pray for wisdom and discernment so that you won't be misled. Are we saved by works? Will what we do or say get us into heaven? Read 7:21–23. 7:28: The people who heard Jesus teach were astonished because He taught with such authority.

Chapter 8: Jesus began healing. Vss 2, 3: A leper; Vss 5–13: One with palsy; Vss 14, 15: Peter's mother in law; Casting out demons in Vs 16; Vss 2–27: Calmed the sea and the disciples. Vss 28–32: Cast out more demons. What happened in 8:34? The people wanted Jesus to leave town. Why? What did they have to fear? Were they afraid that Jesus would see demons in them that needed to be cast out? Why do some people today want to get Jesus out of their lives? We continue to see demon warfare in our day.

Chapter 9: Healings continue. Vss 2–7: A man with palsy. Who did Jesus call in 9:13? Who does He continue to call today? Jesus began preparing the people for His death and ascension in 9:14–17. Vss

18–25: He raised the dead. Did Jesus need to act for a person to be healed? Read 9:20–22. No. The person seeking healing simply needs faith. Jesus continues to offer healing today. Do we have the faith to receive? Vss 27–29 He healed two blind men. Vss 29–34: He healed a man who couldn't speak and was demon possessed. Do Vss 37, 38 apply to us today? Are we willing to be labourers for God?

Chapter 10: Vs 1: To whom did Jesus give power against unclean spirits and to heal? Do we have that power today? Can we have that power today? Vss 2–4: A list of the original twelve disciples. Vss 5, 6: To whom were the twelve sent? Vss 5–-31: Jesus gave instructions to the twelve to prepare them to preach. Jesus told them to be prepared for criticism and persecution.

Chapter 11: Did Jesus quit teaching/preaching after He sent the twelve? See Vs 1. Vss 2–13: John the Baptist was in prison and began to doubt that Jesus was the Son of God. Jesus sent confirmation back to John the Baptist. Then Jesus began bragging about the boldness of John the Baptist. Vs 11: Is Jesus saying that any of us can be greater in heaven than John the Baptist? Vss 18, 19: John was criticized by the leaders because he didn't eat or drink publicly but Jesus was criticized because He did eat and drink publicly. I love Vs 25. How often have we been led by a little child? In their innocence, God protects them and so many times their understanding exceeds ours because they do not attempt to overthink the situation. We try to humanize and theorize situations. They simply trust God. Vss 28–30: A wonderful promise.

Chapter 12: Remember that the Jewish leaders were still trying to obey Old Testament law. Why was Jesus criticized for plucking ears of corn to feed the disciples on the Sabbath? The leaders plotted to destroy Him. Vss 18–21 are prophesied in Isaiah 42:2–4. Vs 24: The Pharisees accused Jesus of getting His power from the devil. How absurd. Is Vs 30 relevant today? Vss 31, 32 address blasphemy against the Holy Ghost. Blasphemy is speaking or acting against God, being disrespectful to God. According to this scripture, we must be very careful today. What is meant by the phrase idle word in Vs 36? Vs 40: Jesus compares His death of three days to the three days that Jonah spent inside the great fish. Vs 42: A reference to the Queen of Sheba from Second Chronicles 9:1 and Luke 11:31. Vss 43–45: Jesus teaches that when an unclean spirit is cast out and the person is cleaning up and changing his ways, that seven more unclean spirits come back with the original spirit to attempt to overtake the person again. Beware. Pray diligently for everyone you know that is trying to follow God. Vss 47–50: Jesus calls everyone who follows Him as His family!

Chapter 13: The parable of the sower. Vs 10: The disciples questioned why Jesus taught in parables. Vs 13: Jesus answered that this is to help people understand. Vss 14, 15 are prophesied in Isaiah 6:9, 10 that people don't understand. Vss 19–23: Jesus explained the parable of the sower. Vss 24–30: Another parable about sowing seed. Vss 31, 32: Yet a third parable of sowing seed. This time it is a tiny seed that grows large. Vs 34: Another parable. Vs 35 is prophesied in Psalm 78:2. Vss 37–50: Jesus continued to explain the parables to the disciples. Look at Vs 44. IF you knew there was great wealth buried in a certain place, would you sell everything you had in order to buy that property? Would you give up everything to be a Christian? Read Vs 49! At the end of the world, the believers will be separated from the non-believers. Where do non-believers go? Read Vs 50. Where to non-believers go? Read Vs 50 again. Vs 54: The people were astonished at Jesus and His teachings. Vss 55, 56 tell us that Jesus had earthly siblings.

Chapter 14: Herod thought that Jesus was John the Baptist come back from the grave. Vss 3–11 tell us that John the Baptist was beheaded in prison and why. Jesus sailed to a desert to be apart after hearing of the beheading of John the Baptist, but a multitude followed Him. The disciples wanted to send the people away but Jesus fed them with five loaves and two fishes. Vs 20: Talk about leftovers! There were twelve baskets full after feeding about 5000 men plus women and children with only five loaves and two fishes. When God feeds us (blesses) he feeds (blesses) abundantly. After feeding the people, He sent them away so He could go to the mountains to pray. Later that night, a storm frightened the disciples in the boat. Jesus walked on water to them. The disciples did not recognize Jesus and were afraid that He was a spirit. Then they recognized His voice. Are we close enough to God to hear Him calm our fears? Peter walked on water but started to sink when he took his eyes off of Jesus and let fear take over. Don't sink. Keep your eyes on Jesus.

CHAPTER 15: The scribes and Pharisees constantly searched for fault in Jesus and the disciples. Vs 2: They even faulted the disciples because they did not always wash their hands. Jesus turned the law back on them about not honoring their parents. Vs 11: What defiles a man? Ever hear the saying about the blind leading the blind? It is Biblical. See Vs 14. Vss 17–20: More teaching about what defiles a person. Vss 22–28: A Gentile woman with great faith asked Jesus to heal her daughter. A great multitude followed Jesus to the mountain. Vs 32: They were three days without food. They were hungry for God's Word! Jesus fed them spiritually and then fed them physically with seven loaves and a few little fishes. There were seven baskets full left over. Oh to be that hungry for God.

CHAPTER 16: Red sky in morning—take warning. Read sky at night—sailors delight. Yes. This is scriptural in Vss 1–4. Vss 13–19: Jesus questioned the disciples about who people thought that He is. Vs 20: Jesus told them not to tell anyone that He is the Christ. Did Jesus insult Peter in Vs 23? Or, did Jesus recognize that Satan was using Peter against Him? Vs 27: The second coming prophesied.

CHAPTER 17: Jesus took Peter, James and John to the mountain. Vs 2 states that Jesus was transfigured (changed, elevated, shining). Moses and Elijah appeared and spoke with Jesus. Vs 5: For the second time, a voice from above announced that Jesus is the beloved Son and that we should hear Him. Again, the disciples experienced fear. Jesus comforted them. Many times we are fearful in new of different situations and Jesus comforts us. Jesus instructed the three disciples in Vs 9 to tell no one about this until after the resurrection. Vss 14–18: Jesus healed a son possessed by a demon. Carefully read Vss 19–21. Why couldn't the disciples cast out that demon? Lack of faith and lack of prayer and fasting. Are these the reasons we don't see more healings today? Does God give His people the same gifts that He gave the disciples? Vss 22, 23: Jesus tried to prepare His disciples for His death and resurrection. Vss 24–27: A unique way to pay taxes.

CHAPTER 18: Once again we see how much Jesus loved little children. We can still learn a lot from children. Read Vs 6. Consider the current abortion laws and now the revamped pedophile laws. FOLKS: America has a lot to answer at the Judgment. Some of our leaders want to pardon pedophiles and abortionists but God says otherwise. Fourteen verses in this chapter alone address the importance of children. Vs 10 tells us that they have their own angels in Heaven. How are we to reconcile differences with other people? Person to Person. Vs 16: If a person won't reconcile one on one, take one or two other people along for a second attempt. Vs 19: If he refuses to reconcile either one on one or with one or two witnesses, take it to the church. Do we follow Biblical teachings in this matter? Have you personally witnessed this approach? Do we have the right to ignore this scripture? Read Vss 19, 20. Jesus says if two or three are together in His name, He will be there. Vs 19 tells us that if two agree, they shall ask and God will grant. Then Peter asked the age-old question of how often we are to forgive someone. Do you have a chart somewhere (even in your mind) counting how many times you have forgiven someone? Is seventy time seven (490) the ultimate number of times we are to forgive someone? Has anyone had to forgive us 490 times? Jesus told a parable in Vss 23–35 about forgiveness. God has forgiven each of us more than 490 times. What would happen if He stopped forgiving us at 490 times? Read Luke 12:48 and let it speak to you about forgiveness. Read Matthew 6: 9–15.

CHAPTER 19: Great multitudes continued to follow Jesus. The Pharisees attempted to trick Jesus with a question about marriage and divorce. Vss 13–15: Jesus blessed the little children. Vss 16–24: A rich young ruler asked Jesus what he needed to do to have eternal life. Jesus told him to keep the commandments and to sell his possessions to give to the poor. Jesus knew the man was proud of his earthly treasures and that giving them up would be difficult. He wouldn't give up his wealth to follow Jesus. Look at Vs 28! The disciples will sit on the thrones in glory and judge the twelve tribes of Israel. What does Vs 29 say? If we give up everything for Jesus's sake, are we guaranteed everlasting life?

CHAPTER 20: A farmer needed laborers in this parable. He agreed to pay all of them the same daily (not hourly) wage whether they worked one hour or all day. The laborers who worked all day were angry. Quite a few years ago, a neighbor gave his heart to God just before he died. A leader in the church I attended stated that the man wouldn't go to heaven. He was angry that someone could repent in the final hours of life and receive eternal life. Vss 17–19: Jesus once again tried to prepare the disciples for His death and resurrection. Vss 20–28: Typical mama. She wanted her boys to rule with Jesus in His kingdom. Jesus told her that she didn't know what she asked. Read Vss 26–28 about the chief being a servant and the greatest becoming a minister. Vss 29–34: Jesus healed the blind.

CHAPTER 21: Up to this point, according to Matthew, Jesus had traveled and preached in the country areas and not in Jerusalem. This chapter opens with the Triumphal entry on Palm Sunday. Jesus rode a donkey – not a horse. This is further proof of His humility. Notice how the people were praising Jesus in this parade. Where is their praise later? Vss 12, 13: Jesus cleared the temple of those buying and selling and cheating folks. Jesus did not stay in Jerusalem at nights in the early part of the week, but traveled back to Bethany. One morning, on His return to Jerusalem, He was hungry and looked on a fig tree for figs. The tree was barren. Jesus commanded the tree to never bear fruit and it withered. Are we bearing fruit?

Jesus was good at answering the chief priests and the elders by asking them questions instead. Jesus told a parable about a man who planted a vineyard. We do not hear this parable very often. The owner sent his servants to receive the fruits of the vineyard but they were stoned and beaten by the renter. The owner sent more servants with the same result. Then the owner sent his son, but the renter killed him also. Is this vineyard a depiction of Israel and their rejection? Read Vss 42–44 and compare to Psalm 118: 22, 23.

CHAPTER 22: The parable of the wedding feast. The king invited the wealthy and the upper class folks but they refused to attend. Then he invited the people of the fringes. They came. Compare Matthew 20:16 and Matthew 22:14. The Pharisees continued to attempt to trap Jesus by asking if it was lawful to pay tribute to Caesar. Read Vs 21. Then the Sadducees came to trap Him with rhetorical (waste of time) questions. Jesus told them in Vs 30 that we will be as the angels of God in heaven. Read First John 3:2 also. Then the Pharisees came at Jesus again. Read Vss 34–46. That put an end to these questions.

CHAPTER 23: Jesus taught the disciples to do as the scribes and Pharisees say and not as they do. He continued to teach the disciples through Vs 22. Jesus pronounced woe to the scribes and Pharisees in Vss 13–39.

CHAPTER 24: Jesus taught the disciples about the end of time. Read this chapter several times and pay close attention to Vs 44. GET READY. BE READY. STAY READY.

CHAPTER 25: Vss 1–12 contain the parable of the sower. Vs 13: GET READY. BE READY. STAY READY. Vss 14–30: The parable of the talents. Vs 26: How did the lord answer the person too timid to use his talent for his Lord (Vss 26–30)? God has given all of us talents and He expects us to use them wisely. Vss 31–46 tell us about dividing the Left from the Right, the goats from the sheep. Read Vss 40 and 45.

CHAPTER 26: Once again Jesus told the disciples of His pending crucifixion. Vss 6-13: A woman anointed Jesus's feet with expensive ointment. Vs 12 tells us that Jesus says that this was in preparation for His burial. Vss 14-16: Judas Iscariot plotted to betray Jesus for money. Vss 17-30: The Last Supper. Even here, Jesus was trying to prepare the disciples for the crucifixion and resurrection. Read Vss 31, 32. Vss 36–46: Jesus took Peter, James and John and left the others with instructions to watch and pray. Then He left Peter, James and John to watch with Him. He went a little farther. Read Vs 39. Can you imagine knowing that He would be crucified and NO other human understood? Peter, James and John went to sleep—totally unaware of things to come. In Vss 39 and 42, Jesus agreed to accept the crucifixion. Three times between Vss 40–45, the disciples slept instead of praying. Vs 49: Jesus was betrayed with a kiss. Vs 50: Even knowing that Judas betrayed Him, Jesus still referred to him as a friend. Read the response of all of the disciples in Vs 56. Vs 57: Jesus's journey through the courts started with Caiphas the high priest. Fake witnesses were sought to testify against Jesus. Vss 67, 68: The folks at court spit on Jesus and hit Him and shoved Him around. Vss 69–75: Peter denied knowing Jesus three times as prophesied by Jesus.

CHAPTER 27: The next morning (after court with Caiphas) Jesus was delivered to Pilate, the governor. Judas threw down the thirty pieces of silver and hanged himself. Pilate did not want to pronounce the death sentence on Jesus so he offered to free either Jesus or Barabbus a murderer. Pilate should have listened to his wife (Vs 19) but he let the people choose. Once again, Pilate asked in Matthew Chapter 27, Verse 22: "What shall I do then with Jesus which is called Christ? They all say unto him, Let him be crucified." Still today, it is crucial that we pray for our leaders. Vss 26–35: Jesus was whipped, stripped, dressed in a scarlet robe, mocked and crowned with thorns, spit upon, hit in the head, given vinegar to drink and was crucified. Vs 50: Jesus died. Vss 51–54: The temple veil was torn from top to bottom—not by human hands. There was an earthquake. The bodies of the saints came out of the graves. After the resurrection, these saints appeared to many people. Vs 54: The centurion accepted that Jesus is the Son of God. Jesus's body was placed in a borrowed tomb. Vss 62–66: The chief priests and Pharisees went to Pilate to demand that guards be sent to the tomb. They also sealed the tomb.

CHAPTER 28: Two women went to the tomb early on Sunday morning. There was another earthquake. An angel rolled back the stone and sat on it. This scared the guards. The angel told the women to take a look into the empty tomb and then to go and tell the others that Jesus is risen and that He had gone to Galilee. Along the way they met Jesus. Jesus also told them to go to tell the disciples and for them to go to Galilee. Vss 11–15: The guards were given large amounts of money to tell people that the body had been stolen. Vss 16–20: The eleven disciples found Jesus and worshipped Him, but some doubted. Vss 18–20: The Great Commission.

LESSON THIRTY-FIVE
MARK

Mark did not begin this gospel with the birth of Jesus. Instead, he started with the fulfillment of the prophecy about John the Baptist. John the Baptist taught baptism, repentance and the remission of sins and he taught about the Holy Ghost (1:8). John also was blessed to baptize Jesus in the Jordan River. Mark also relays the appearance of a dove and the voice from heaven saying that Jesus is the Beloved Son. Mark just gives two verses to the time that Jesus was in the wilderness and tempted of Satan. What was Jesus's message in 1:15? We see four disciples chosen, Jesus casting out unclean spirits, the healing of Peter's mother in law, healing many other folks. At this point Jesus was famous and crowds followed Him. Were they honestly listening or just curious? Are we honestly listening?

Chapter 2: Vss 2–12 tell of four friends who brought a man to Jesus. When they could not get into the house by the door, they tore up the roof and lowered him to Jesus. Once again, the scribes tried to stir up trouble by questioning Jesus. Vs 14: The calling of Levi (Matthew) at the toll gate. He was a publican (tax collector). Vss 16, 17: Jesus ate with publicans and sinners. The scribes and Pharisees thought this was terrible. Read Vs 17 again. Are churches for perfect people or for people who need forgiveness? Already in 2:19, Jesus began to teach the disciples that He would not always be with them physically. Mark Chapter 2, Verse 28: "Therefore the Son of man is Lord also of the Sabbath".

Chapter 3: The Pharisees sought to destroy Jesus. The healings and teachings continue. Jesus added disciples. Why? Vss 14, 15. They are named in Vss 16–19.

Chapter 4: Jesus taught in parables. (Vss 2–11). Vs 12: Is this true today as it was in the days when Jesus was physically here on earth? Even Isaiah prophesied this in Isaiah 6:9. Jesus explained the parable in Vss 13–20. Vss 37–41: Fear. What did Jesus do? In Mark Chapter 4, Verse 39 "Peace, Be Still" Jesus said to the sea. Fear is running rampant today. Almost daily, friends comment that they are not sleeping well because of fear. Please review Psalm 4:8. God wants our faith and our trust. He tells us to have peace and to be still just as He told the stormy sea.

Chapter 5: Jesus cast out many demons. The demons went into swine and the swine ran over the cliff into the sea. What did Jesus tell the man who was previously possessed? (Vs 19.). A missionary (Vs 20). Healings continue as Jesus teaches.

Chapter 6: Vs 4. A teacher, preacher, prophet has no honor in his hometown. Vs 6: Jesus marveled at the unbelief of the people. Vs 7: The 12 were sent 2 by 2 without extra clothing or money. Would we go today without provisions? What did they preach? Repentance (Vs 12). Mark tells us about the beheading of John the Baptist (Vss 14–29). Vss 35–44 tell us about the feeding of the 5000 plus women and children.

Chapter 7: The scribes and Pharisees were critical of the disciples because they did not wash their hands. Jesus told them in Vs 7 that they were only giving lip service-not obeying God. Jesus taught about defilement in Vss 14–23.

Chapter 8: Feeding the 4000. When Jesus blesses, there are no limits. Even after witnessing these miracles, the disciples did not believe or trust fully (Vss 14–21). Vss 27–30: Jesus inquired if the disciples knew Him. Read and ponder Vss 36, 37.

Chapter 9: The Transfiguration of Jesus. The appearance of Elijah and Moses on the Mountain. Vs 9: Jesus told Peter, James and John not to tell anyone about what they witnessed until after the resurrection. Vss 17–29: A young man delivered of an evil spirit. Vs 29 tells us that this only comes through prayer and fasting. Vss 30–32: Jesus taught the disciples that He would be killed and then arise on the third day. Vss 36, 37: Jesus showed how He loves children. Vss 44, 46, 48: Where is the worm that does not die and where is the fire that is never quenched? Read 9:43.

Chapter 10: Vss 4–12: Jesus taught about marriage. Vss 13–16: Jesus blessed the little children. Vss 17–27: The story of giving all for salvation. Vss 33, 34: Jesus once again tried to prepare the disciples for His death and resurrection. What is Jesus's purpose? Vs 45. What made blind Bartimaeus see?

Chapter 11: Preparation and the Triumphal Entry into Jerusalem. Vss 15–18: Jesus cleared/cleansed the temple. Vss 23–26: Read this wonderful teaching about faith.

Chapter 12: Vss 1–13: Compare this to Matthew Chapter 21. I think that THE LIVING BIBLE published by Tyndale makes this more clear to us. It tells us that the Jewish leaders were the tenant farmers who did not want to give God what was due Him. They had plotted/planned/schemed to destroy Jesus. Jesus is our cornerstone. Vss 14–17: Giving what is owed. Vss 18–27: Once again, the Sadducees attempted to trick Jesus. They were a Jewish religious party but did not accept Jesus's or God's power. I have heard basically this same question about whose spouse will one be in Heaven if one has been married more than once. Read Vss 25–27. The hypocritical scribes are described in Vss 38–40. Vss 41–44: The widow's mite.

Chapter 13: Jesus warned about false teachers and of happenings before the end of time. He also taught that they (we) will be persecuted for His sake. We are not to plan what to speak but to let the Holy Ghost speak for us. Vss 12, 13: We have seen this before and continue to see this today. Read the promise in 13:13. Endure! VS 19: There will be troubles more than ever before. Vs 20: God will shorten the time so that the chosen may be saved. Vss 24–27: After these troubled times, the Son of man will come with His angels to gather the elect. Vss 32–37: WATCH! PRAY! BE READY!

Chapter 14: Jesus was anointed with costly ointment. Vs 8: Jesus said this was in preparation for His death. How did Mary grasp this when the disciples didn't? Jesus us our Passover lamb. Vss 12–26: Preparation for and participation in the Last Supper (Our basis for communion). Vs 28: Jesus told the disciples that He would return to Galilee after He arose. They did not grasp that concept. Vs 34: Jesus told Peter, James and John that His soul was sorrowful. Did they understand? Vs 36: Jesus asked God to stop His death but then agreed to God's will. Three times, Jesus returned to Peter, James and John after He prayed. Every time He found them sleeping. Vss 56–58: The testimony of the false witnesses did not even agree. Vss 63–65: The high priest tore His clothes, the people spit on Him, hit Him and shoved Him. Peter denied Jesus three times. How many times do we deny Him?

Chapter 15: Jesus was taken to Pilate and was accused of many things by the high priests. Vs 10: Why did the chief priests deliver Jesus to Pilate? Envy. They even talked the crowd into demanding that Barabbas, a murderer, be released instead of Jesus. All of this was foretold by the prophets in the Old Testament. Vss 25–38: Jesus was scourged, crowned with thorns, mocked, hit, spit upon, crucified. The earth was dark from noon until three PM while Jesus was on the cross. Vs 37: Jesus cried out in a loud voice and died. Vs 38: The veil of the temple was torn from top to bottom. First Kings 6:2 tells us that the veil was thirty cubits (about forty-five feet) tall. Vs 39: A centurion at the cross realized that Jesus is the Son of God. Vss 43–46: Joseph of Arimathea donated his tomb (sepulcher) for Jesus's body.

Chapter 16: Early Sunday morning, three women went to the tomb. The stone had been rolled away. An angel was inside the tomb and told the ladies that Jesus is risen and had gone to Galilee just as He had told the disciples in Mark 14:28. Did the people believe this when Mary Magdalene told them? (Vs 11). Jesus appeared to Mary Magdalene, (Vs 9), to two others (Vs 12), to the eleven (Vs 14). Vss 15–20: The great commission and the ascension. Do Vss 15–18 apply to us today?

LESSON THIRTY-SIX
LUKE

Written by Luke, the physician. Refer to Acts 1:1, 2. Acts was also written by Luke. The gospel of Luke was written to verify the gospels of Matthew and Mark (Vs 4). As a doctor, Luke writes more about the birth of John the Baptist and the birth of Jesus. Vs 5 tells us that Zacharias was a priest and that his wife Elisabeth was from the priestly line of Aaron. Both were blameless (Vs 6). Elisabeth was old and barren (Vs 11). An angel, Gabriel, appeared at the altar while Zacharias was burning incense (Vs 19). Zacharias, like Joseph a few months later, was afraid. Gabriel told Zacharias not to be afraid, that they would have a son and he was to be named John (Vs 13). John would be filled with the Holy Ghost while in Elisabeth's womb. (Vs15). John would prepare people to receive God (Vss 16, 17). Six months later, Gabriel appeared to Mary (Vs 26) and told Mary that she had found favor with God (Vs 30) and that she would have a son of the Holy Ghost (Vs 35) and to call His name Jesus (Vs 31). Then Gabriel told Mary that her cousin Elisabeth was pregnant. Mary was also of the priestly line of Aaron. Read Verse 37! Still true! Mary went to visit Elisabeth. When Elisabeth heard Mary's greeting, the baby John leaped within her womb and Elisabeth was filled with the Holy Ghost (Vs 41). Vss 42–55: Elisabeth praised God! John was born. Eight days later, he was circumcised and his father named him John. Then Zacharias was able to speak (Vs 64). Vs 67: Zacharias was filled with the Holy Ghost and prophesied (Vss 67–79). Vs 76: John would be a prophet helping to prepare the Way of the Lord.

Chapter 2: Tax time. In those days, you traveled to the city of your family's origin to pay your taxes and for the census. Thus, Joseph and Mary traveled to Bethlehem because they were descendants of David. While in Bethlehem, Mary gave birth to Jesus. Why was Jesus placed in a manger (Vs 7)? Angels visited some shepherds in the fields of Judea and told them that a Saviour was born in Bethlehem (Vs 11). The shepherds were curious and quickly went into Bethlehem to see the Saviour. Did they keep the wonderful news to themselves? No (Vss 17, 18). Vs 22: Joseph and Mary took Baby Jesus to Jerusalem after His circumcision to offer sacrifices. According to Matthew Chapter 2, Herod was in Jerusalem when the wise men found him. Remember that. Vs 39: They returned to

Nazareth. There is a popular theory that Jesus was two years old when the wise men came to see Him. I disagree. 1). Why would they go to Bethlehem to see him when His family went to Jerusalem each year (Vs 41)? 2). Is it because of Matthew 2: Vss 8, 9, 11? That scripture says young child. Read Luke 2:27. This refers to Jesus as a child and we know that Jesus was only eight days old (or slightly more) when they went to Jerusalem for the circumcision. If you have documentation that Jesus was two years old or older when the wise men came, please share it with me. Vss 42–52: Jesus at twelve was in the temple listening to and answering questions of the teachers.

Chapter 3: The ministry of John the Baptist. Vs 15: The people questioned who Jesus Is. Read John's answer in Vss 16–18. Because of his stand for Jesus, John was imprisoned. How old was Jesus when He began preaching? (Vs 23). Vss 34–38: The genealogy of Jesus back to Adam. Who was Adam (Vs 38)?

Chapter 4: Jesus was in the wilderness. Satan attempted to trick Jesus. Where did Jesus go when He left the wilderness (Vs 9)? Then where did Jesus go (Vs 14)? Read Jesus's calling in Vss 18–21. The people doubted. Jesus gave them scriptural evidence that prophets weren't accepted in their own country. What was their response (Vss28–30)? Was Jesus accepted in Capernaum (Vss 31–37)?

Chapter 5: Jesus helped the fisherman on the Lake of Gennesaret. Simon, Andrew, James and John then became His Fishers of Men. Jesus continued to heal, to forgive sin. Levi (Matthew) was called to be a disciple (Vss 27, 28). Even this early in His ministry, He began to prepare the disciples for his leaving.

Chapter 6: Vss 7, 11: The scribes and Pharisees sought to find fault in Jesus. Vss 13–16: A list of the twelve disciples (later called Apostles). Vss 17–19: How many were healed? Vss 20–49: A short version of the Sermon on the Mount.

Chapter 7: Jesus returned to Capernaum. Vss 2–10: The Centurion's servant was healed. Vss 11–16: A dead man was raised. Vss 24–29: Jesus taught the people about John the Baptist. Vss 36–50: Jesus was invited to a Pharisee's house (Simon) for a meal. There He was anointed with ointment. Read how Jesus answered the accusations of Simon and the guests.

Chapter 8: Who helped support Jesus's ministry financially (Vss 2, 3)? Jesus taught in parables and then explained most of them. Jesus slept in the midst of a storm. Then He cast demons out of a man. There were so many that a herd of swine ran violently over the cliff after the demons went into them. Vss 41–56: Jairus's daughter was raised from the dead.

Chapter 9: Power and Authority given to the twelve to teach, preach, and heal. When the twelve returned, Jesus took them to Bethsaida. There the 5000 men plus women and children were fed (Vss 22–27). Jesus taught the disciples of what was to come. Vss 28–36: Jesus's transfiguration.

Chapter 10: Vs 1: Jesus appointed seventy men to go out two by two to preach and teach. Why (Vs 2)? How (Vss3–16)? Then read their report and Jesus's reply in Vss 17–24. Who is our neighbor (Vss 29–37)? Does this apply to us today?

Chapter 11: Vss 2–4: Part of the Lord's Prayer. Vss 5–13: Jesus taught about giving and receiving. Vs 29: Many people gathered. Jesus once again connects Old Testament Jonah to New Testament Jesus (Luke 24:46, Acts 10:40). I don't see Jonah in the birth line of either Matthew Chapter 1 or Luke Chapter 3 but this provides another connection between the Old and New Testaments (Vss 29–32). Vss 37–44: Jesus was invited to dine with a Pharisee. Vs 38 tells us that the Pharisee was upset because Jesus did not wash His hands. Jesus taught the gathering that inner cleanliness is more important than outward washing. He continued to point out the inequities of the hypocritical scribes and Pharisees. Vss 46–52: Jesus pronounced woe on the crooked lawyers, holding them responsible for the corruption. Were the lawyers, scribes or Pharisees happy? No. They plotted even more to accuse Jesus.

Chapter 12: So many people gathered that they were crushing each other (Vs 1). Vss 1–12: Jesus taught His disciples (and us) to watch out for the hypocrites, that everything will eventually be brought to light. Vs 12: Let the Holy Ghost teach you what to say. Confess Christ. Jesus taught a parable about a rich man who planned to build bigger warehouses so he could keep everything to himself. Read and heed Vss 20, 21. Then He taught about God's provisions. Read Vs 34. Vss 35–59 GET READY! BE READY! STAY READY! **HE IS** COMING! Read the second part of Vs 48. We have been given much!

Chapter 13: Vs 5 is clear and simple. Repentance is required. We have often been taught that the fig tree symbolizes Israel. Vss 6–9: Is Jesus talking about God sending a husbandman (Jesus) to work with the barren tree (Israel) for three years (the length of time that Jesus preached)? Vss 11–17: Jesus healed a crippled woman on the Sabbath day. Once again, the leaders condemned Him. Vss 18–21: Jesus taught that the kingdom of God is like a small thing (a mustard seed or grains of yeast) that will grow and flourish into something big (large tree or loaves of risen bread). Vss 23–30: Jesus taught that not everyone who has been with Him will enter heaven. Vss 31–35: Here come the Pharisees again, telling Jesus to get out and that Herod would kill Him. Jesus called Herod a fox (sly, sneaky). He refers to His death and resurrection on the third day.

Chapter 14: Once again, Jesus ate at the home of a Pharisee. Even though He knew they hated Him and were looking for ways to attack Him, He used every opportunity to witness and teach. Vss 7–11: A parable teaching not to elevate (exalt) self. Vss 16–4: A parable of a wedding feast. Many made excuses why they could not go. A wedding feast is a glorious time of celebrating in all cultures, so everyone can relate to this parable. Jesus is the Bride of the Church and we are invited to celebrate with Him. Don't make excuses. Vss 26–35: Jesus teaches that there are costs to following Him. Salvation is FREE but we must plan, study and be prepared for attacks from others.

Chapter 15: Look at His audience in Vs 1. Publicans and sinners. Just everyday people like us. Hungry to get close to Jesus, hungry to learn. Vs 2: Jealousy—a terribly destructive force. Vss 4–10: Parable of the lost sheep and the lost coin. Read Vs 10! The parable of the Prodigal son (Vss 11–32). God wants us no matter who we are or what we have done.

Chapter 16: What is a steward? A person who looks after property or is responsible for something/a manager/an official/someone who manages or administers. In this story, I would say he was probably the accountant. The rich man heard rumors that the steward was dishonest. The rich man told him to get his paperwork in order and that he was going to be fired. The accountant cooked up a scheme to cheat his boss even more. He instructed the debtors to tear up their contracts and to write new ones for lesser amounts. Many today would see this as a wise move, but dishonesty is dishonesty. The people who operate like this do not think in godly ways. Vs 13: You can't serve God and money. This hits home with many of us. Vss 15–17: God knows what is in our hearts, no matter how we appear outwardly. We may be honored by people, but still be an abomination to God. Vss 19–31: The story of Lazarus, a beggar.

Chapter 17: Another lesson on forgiveness (Vss 1–4). Vss 11–19: The healing of the ten lepers. Only one thanked Jesus. Vss 20–37: No one knows God's timing of the end.

Chapter 18: A parable about an unrighteous judge who protected his people. Vss 10–14: The publican at prayer compared to the Pharisee praying. Jesus loves children. We see this repeatedly in the scriptures (Vss 15–17). Vss 18–30: The parable of the rich, young ruler. Vss 31–34: Jesus told the disciples that He would be mocked, spit upon, scourged and put to death but they still did not understand.

Chapter 19: Zacchaeus—a rich tax collector. He was short in stature but wanted to see Jesus. He even climbed a tall tree because there was a large crowd and he couldn't see around them. Vs 15: Jesus looked up and saw Zacchaeus and invited himself to Zacchaeus's house. Zacchaeus was delighted, but the crowd murmured. Did Jesus tell Zacchaeus to restore the falsely obtained money four-fold or did conviction hit Zacchaeus in the presence of the Lord? Zacchaeus was saved that very day (Vss 9, 10). Vs 11: The disciples believed that the kingdom of God would begin immediately as they approached Jerusalem, so Jesus taught them again with a parable about a nobleman going away to be crowned king. He gave one pound to each of his servants to invest while he was gone. Upon his return, one had gained ten pounds, one had gained five pounds, one hid his pound. The nobleman took the hidden pound and gave it to the servant who had earned ten pounds. Why (Vs 26)? As Jesus neared Jerusalem, He sent two disciples for a young colt. He wept over Jerusalem (Vs 41). Why? Because the people had rejected God. Then He cleared the temple. Once again, the chief priests and scribes tried to destroy Jesus because the people were quite attentive to Him. Does Vs 46 apply to us today?

Chapter 20: Jesus taught in the temple (Vs 1). He did not tell the priests and scribes the origin of his authority (Vs 8). Jesus IS our Cornerstone—the one Who was rejected (Vs 17).

Chapter 21: As recorded in Matthew Chapter 24 and again in Mark Chapter 13, Jesus taught about the Great Tribulation. Read Vs 36. There IS a glorious hope.

Chapter 22: Jesus prepared for the Last Supper for the twelve disciples and Himself. Compare Mark 15:23 to Luke 22:18. Vss 24–30: Which is greater—the servant or the master? Jesus addressed this topic many times. As I read these verses, I thought about Jesus as a servant. 1). He did His Father's will, 2). He died for our sins, 3). He washed the feet of the disciples, 4). He was so humble, 5). He was compassionate, 6). Even on the cross, He was obedient to His calling and forgave the repentant thief (Luke 23:43). On the other hand, the disciples called Him Master, the rich young ruler called Him Master. The ten lepers called Him Master. Jesus was both, the master and the servant. Are we too proud to serve? Vss 31–34: Jesus knew that Satan desperately wanted Peter. Peter was a strong character, a born leader. Read Matthew 16:23 again. Jesus was not rebuking Peter. He was rebuking Satan. We still have that privilege today to call Satan by name and rebuke him. Do not let Satan destroy you, your family or your country. Read First Peter 5:8. Jesus loved Peter. He knew that once Peter completely yielded to God, he would be the rock. In Vs 32, Jesus told Peter that He prayed for him. The prayer was for a strong faith and that Peter would truly be a rock for the other disciples. Peter preached on the Day of Pentecost (Acts 2:14–41). Look at the results (Acts 2:41). Jesus prayed in the garden (Vs 42). He had asked Peter, James and John to pray for Him, but they fell asleep. An angel came to Jesus in the garden (22:43).

Chapter 23: Vss 1, 2: False accusations. How did Jesus answer in Mark 12:14–17? Read Matthew 17:24–27. Vss 3–25: Neither Pilate nor Herod found reason for the death of Jesus. But, they gave in to the crowd. Jesus was crucified.

Chapter 24: Ladies from Galilee went to the tomb early on Sunday Morning. The stone had been rolled away! The tomb was empty! Two angels told the ladies that He is risen! They went to tell the disciples. Peter went to see for himself. Two of the disciples were walking to Emmaus. Jesus appeared to them. They did not recognize Him. He preached a long sermon to them (Vs 27). How did they recognize Him (Vss 30, 31)? Even though it was late in the day (Vs 29), they returned immediately to Jerusalem to join the disciples and other believers. See Vs 36! Jesus appeared and spoke with them. They were terrified. Jesus showed them His hands and feet, then asked for food. Vs 44: Jesus told them that He is the fulfillment of the law of Moses, the Prophets and the Psalms. Where did Jesus tell them to stay until they received power from on high (Vs 49)? Vss 50–53: Blessing. Ascension. Worship.

LESSON THIRTY-SEVEN

JOHN

This gospel is written by John the beloved apostle. Why (John 20:31)? John does not tell about the birth of Jesus other than in Vs 14. Why? Because John wanted everyone to know that Jesus was with God from the beginning of time. Read Genesis Chapter 1, John 1:1–5, John 1:10, John 8:58, Ephesians 3:9, Hebrews 1:1, 2. Vss 15–36: John the Baptist testified about Jesus.

Chapter 2: Jesus's first miracle (Vs 11) was turning water into wine at a wedding. Jesus already was preparing for the crucifixion and the resurrection (Vss 19–22).

Chapter 3: Vs 3 is still true today. This is important. Jesus repeats it in Vss 15, 16.

Chapter 4: Who actually baptized those that believed in Jesus (Vs 2)? Jesus was a humble man. Even though His first mission was to the Children of Israel, He sat down and talked to a Samaritan woman (Vs 9). Vss 10–14: Living water. What type of people does God the Father seek to worship Him (Vs 23)? How do we worship God (Vs 24)? Jesus told the Samaritan woman that He is Jesus, The Christ (Vs 26). She went to find her men and they came to find Jesus (Vss 28–30). She was a missionary (Vss39–42). Jesus's second miracle (Vss 46–54). Who has the power to judge (Vss 22, 26, 27)? How (Vs 30)?

Chapter 5: Jesus began healing and forgiving people. Vss 19–47: Honour the Father and the Son.

Chapter 6: Vs 33: The Bread of Life. Who is the Bread of Life (Vss 35, 48, 51)? What is the Father's will (Vs 40)?

Chapter 7: Jesus went secretly (not taking His disciples) to the Feast of the Tabernacles. He taught in the temple (Vs 14). He had the rulers in a quandary. They finally gave up for the day and went home.

Chapter 8: The woman caught in adultery. Why didn't the Pharisees arrest Jesus that day (Vs 20)? Where was the man caught in adultery? What makes us free (Vs 32)? Jesus did not cut any slack on the Jews (Vss 44–48).

Chapter 9: Jesus healed a man who had been blind since birth. The Pharisees accused Jesus of sin because He healed on the Sabbath. In Vs 16 they even called Jesus a sinner. When the Pharisees questioned the man's parents about the miracle, they pleaded ignorance. Why (Vs 22)? Vs 27: The man asked the Pharisees if they would like to be disciples (Vs 27). He continued to testify to them (Vss 24–34). The man became a believer.

Chapter 10: The parable of the good shepherd. The sheep know His voice and follow Him. Are we close enough to OUR Shepherd to hear and recognize His voice and to follow Him? Somewhere in my history, I heard that the shepherd would actually lie in the doorway of the sheep fold. That would explain Vs 9. Why did Jesus agree to be our Shepherd (Vs 10)? Vs 15 says that Jesus would lay down His life for His sheep. He did! Read Vs 18. Jesus could have refused to go to the cross. What time of year was the Feast of the Dedication (Vs 22)?

Chapter 11: Remember Mary who anointed Jesus's feet with expensive ointment in Mark 14:3? Her brother, Lazarus, was sick. Mary and Martha sent for Jesus to come. Jesus was their friend (Vs 5). Even though the Jews had attempted to stone Jesus, He went anyway. In Vs 14 Jesus told the disciples that Lazarus was dead. Doubting Thomas went along to see. When Jesus got to Bethany, Lazarus had been in the tomb for four days. Plain-spoken Martha told Jesus (Vs 21) that her brother would not have died if Jesus had come when He was first notified. But, in Vss 22 and 27 she showed her faith. Even Mary told Jesus in Vs 32 that Lazarus would not have died if Jesus had come sooner. Jesus loved this family so much that "Jesus wept" according to John Chapter 11, Verse 35. Jesus called Lazarus to come out of the tomb. Lazarus came out! Some of the people believed that day (Vs 45) but some went to tattle. Why were the Pharisees and Jewish leaders afraid of Jesus (Vss 47, 48)? Caiaphas, the high priest in Matthew 26:57 prophesied that Jesus would die (Vs 51).

Chapter 12: John's report of Mary and the expensive ointment (Vss 9–11) tells us that the chief priests wanted to put Lazarus to death also. In Vs 24, Jesus compared Himself to a seed that falls into the ground and dies, then produces a lot of fruit. Vs 28: Jesus is glorified by a voice from heaven. The people were confused when they heard this. Some thought it was thunder. Some thought it was an angel. Read Vs 32. Thank you Lord for this promise. Vs 42 tells us that many of the rulers believed but Vss 42, 43 tell us they would not confess this for fear of losing their place in the synagogue AND because they loved the praise of man more than the praise of God.

Chapter 13: Jesus washed the feet of His disciples—even the feet of Judas Iscariot. Vss 34, 35: Jesus commands us to love one another.

Chapter 14: Jesus continued to prepare the disciples for His death, resurrection and ascension. Jesus promised them (and promises us) the Comforter who will abide with us forever. The Comforter is The Holy Ghost (Vs 26).

Chapters 15–17: Jesus continued to teach and to prepare the eleven disciples. He is also teaching us. Why does Jesus teach (15:11)? Why must Jesus leave (16:7)? Jesus prayed for His disciples (17:9). What does He pray for them and for us (17:15–26)?

Chapters 18, 19: Jesus was betrayed in the garden by Judas Iscariot. The officers bound Jesus and took Him to the courts. (First to Annas, then to Caiaphas, then the judgment hall to Pilate). Pilate did not want the responsibility but he bowed to the demands of the people. When I think of priests, I think of religious leaders. But, during Jesus's ministry, the chief priests found fault with Jesus. Vs 19:6 indicates that the chief priests were the main ones who cried for Him to be crucified. 19:11: Where does all power derive? Pilate made a sign and had it put on the cross in Hebrew, Greek and Latin (19:19, 20). Why didn't they tear up Jesus's coat (19:24 and Psalms 22:18). Why didn't they break His legs like they did the legs of the two thieves (19:31–36, Psalms 34:20)?

Chapter 20: Mary Magdalene and other ladies, Peter and John went to the tomb early Sunday Morning. Jesus was not there (Vss 1–9). Peter and John left, but Mary stayed a while. When Jesus spoke to her, she knew Him (Vs 16). Jesus appeared to the disciples and breathed the Holy Ghost upon them (Vss 19–32). Eight days later, He appeared to them again (Vss 26–31).

Chapter 21: Jesus appeared to Peter, Thomas, Nathanael, James and John and to two other disciples while they fished in the sea of Tiberias. Why did Jesus ask Peter three times if he loved Jesus (Vss 15–17)? Was it because Peter had denied Him three times?

Who wrote the Gospel of John (Vs 24, 25)?

This is the end of the four Gospels. Our next lessons will be in Acts as we learn about the early church.

LESSON THIRTY-EIGHT

ACTS

This book was written by Luke telling about the early church and its missions (Luke 1:1–3 and Acts 1:1–4). Is Acts 1:7, 8 relevant today? Do we receive power through the Holy Ghost? Where did the Ascension occur (Vs 1:12)? Who was in the Upper Room (Vss 13–15)? Vs 26: Matthias was chosen to join the eleven disciples/ (apostles).

Chapter 2: Fifty days after Jesus's death, the Holy Spirit came like a mighty wind. According to Acts 1:3, the Upper Room group was praying together with one accord for ten days before the Holy Spirit came. Are we willing to pray with one accord for that long? The multitude was amazed that these simple Galileans could speak in their languages (Vss 6–12). This had been prophesied in Joel 2:28–32. Who preached the first Holy Ghost sermon (Vs 2:14)? Did the multitude respond (Vs 41)? Did the believers just get together randomly to pray (Vss 46, 47)?

Chapter 3: Peter and John healed a lame man in the name of Jesus (Vss 4–7). Peter addressed the crowd boldly (Vss 22–26).

Chapter 4: Already persecution came to Peter and john. They were jailed overnight (Vss 1–3). But! How many people believed that day (Vs 4)? The next day, Peter and John were taken to council and questioned. Again, Peter spoke boldly and gave Jesus the glory. The council forbade them to mention Jesus again. Did they (Vss 19, 20)? Read Psalm 2:1, 2. Then read Acts 4:24–26. They prayed for boldness for healing, for signs and wonders (Vss 29–30). Read the result in Vs 31. We need to pray today for boldness and wisdom.

Chapter 5: Ananias and Sapphira sold some property and kept part of the proceeds. Their sin was not in the withholding of the money, but in lying to the Holy Ghost (Vss 3, 4). What was their punishment? Death. On the spot. Great fear (Vs 11) came upon the people. What an object lesson. What happened in Vs 14? Healing continued (Vss 15, 16). The high priests were upset with the apostles and put them in prison. They angel of the Lord told them to go speak in the temple. The angel opened the prison doors for them (Vss 19, 20). The apostles taught in the temple (Vs 21). The officers found the prison locked up tightly but it was empty (Vs 23). The officers went to the temple and took the apostles to council. What was their reply (Vss 29–32)? Read Gamaliel's speech (Vss 34–39). Pay special attention to Vs 39. Vs 40: The apostles were beaten. Vs 41: The apostles rejoiced to be counted worthy to suffer for God. Did they stop teaching/preaching (Vs 42)?

Chapter 6: Here comes the socialism doctrine from the Greeks (Vs 1). Think about it. A woman in our own congregation said that socialism is biblical. Read this chapter carefully. This was a play to change the ministry from repentance and salvation to socialism and works. Woe. Woe. Today, we need to reconsider our values. What did the apostles do? They remembered the last words of Jesus before His ascension commanding them to preach the gospel (Matthew 28:18–20, Mark 16:15–20, Luke 24:45–53). This has not changed. They chose seven honest men, full of the Holy Ghost and wisdom to help the widows (Vss 3–8). Read Vs 4 again. The apostles prayed continually for these helpers and continued their teaching/preaching as Christ had commanded them. Read Deuteronomy 1: 13. Moses chose wise men to hear the people's problems so that he could continue his calling. This is Old Testament confirmed in the New Testament. I have always told my class that we can make connections from Old Testament to New Testament to Today for instructions from God.

Chapter 7: Read Stephen's reply to the council (Vss 2–53). Stephen reviewed the Old Testament from Abraham to their current time. Are we that familiar with the Bible that we could do this? Do we see the ultimate CONNECTION between Old Testament to New Testament to now? The council was mad. Vss 55–60: Stephen's testimony, his legacy. He saw Jesus standing to receive him! This is the only reference in the Bible that Jesus was standing to receive a person.

Chapter 8: Saul is introduced to us (Vss 1, 3). Philip went to Samaria to preach. Peter and John traveled to Samaria as prayer warriors. The Holy Ghost came upon the people when Peter and John laid hands on them. Simon, a former sorcerer, wanted that power also and tried to buy it (Vss18, 19). Peter discerned this request (Vss 20–24). Philip was sent to Gaza to preach to an Ethiopian eunuch. It was not a coincidence that the man was reading a prophecy of Jesus in Isaiah chapter 53. He believed and was baptized.

Chapter 9: Here came Saul again—threatening and persecuting the believers (Vss 1, 2). But he saw the light and heard the voice of Jesus. He was blinded by that light (Vs 7). An obedient believer in Damascus (Vss 10–18) went to preach to Saul. The result (Vss 17–31)? Think about Saul after he became Paul. God works in mysterious ways. Peter prayed for Dorcas and God raised her from the dead (Vss 32–43).

Chapter 10: The visions of Cornelius and Peter. Peter's sermon to Cornelius and his household (Vss 34–43). This is our first record of a Gentile receiving the Holy Ghost.

Chapter 11: The apostles were upset that Jesus was being shared with the Gentiles. Peter told them about his vision. Vs 18: They were glad that Peter obeyed. Who was Barnabas? He was not one of the original twelve disciples. Is he the man referenced in Acts 4:36, 37? Is he the same Barnabas who took Saul to the apostles in Acts 9:26–31? See Vs 24. A good man, full of the Holy Ghost and faith. He was sent to Tarsus to find Saul. He found him and took him to Antioch for one year to teach the people in Antioch. It was in Antioch that the believers were called Christians for the first time (Vs 26).

Chapter 12: We have several references to Herod in the Bible. Matthew chapter 2 tells of a Herod who was the king of Judea when Jesus was born. Matthew chapter 14 tells of a Herod who had John the Baptist beheaded. Acts chapter 12 tells us about a Herod who killed James, the brother of John the Beloved and that he planned to kill Peter. This Herod was smitten by an angel of the Lord and was eaten by worms. Is the Herod in Matthew 2 the same Herod in Matthew 14 and in Acts 12? The Herod in Acts 12 hated Jesus and tried to stop any mention of Him. Read 12:5–24 to learn how Peter escaped. Vs 25: John Mark joined Saul and Barnabas.

Chapter 13: The Holy Ghost put Saul and Barnabas together for missionary work (Vss 1–3). Vs 9: Saul's name was changed to Paul. Vss 14–52 give us Paul's sermon to the Jews and to the Gentiles.

Chapter 14: Persecution continued. Paul and Barnabas went to Lystra and preached. When a crippled man was healed, the crowd attempted to make gods of Paul and Barnabas. Paul and Barnabas refused this and preached even harder. They stoned Paul (Vs 19). Paul got up and started preaching again. Then he went back to Lystra. They prayed and fasted with the elders (Vss 22, 23). Then they traveled to Antioch and stayed a while.

Chapter 15: The people questioned whether the non-Jewish believers required circumcision. Peter addressed this and solved the issue (Vss 7–11). The apostles and the elders sent Judas and Silas and Paul and Barnabas to Antioch. They also sent letters (Vss 22–29). Paul and Barnabas agreed to retrace their journey to check on the new congregations. Barnabas wanted to take John Mark also, but disagreed with Paul. Paul and Barnabas switched teams. Barnabas took John Mark, and Paul took Silas.

Chapter 16: Paul met Timothy. Timothy knew the scriptures (Second Timothy 3:14.15). Paul invited Timothy on a missionary journey. People believed. Churches were strengthened and grew (Vs 5). Why didn't they go to Asia (Vs 6)? In Troas, Paul received the Macedonian call. There he met Lydia, a worshipper. She invited Paul and Silas to her home. Paul cast a demon out of a young woman in the name of Jesus (Vss 16–19). Paul and Silas were beaten and jailed (Vss 19–24) because of this. What did Paul and Silas do (Vs 25)? There was an earthquake, a prison conversion and hospitality. Paul and Silas were released (Vss 26–40).

Chapter 17: In Chapter 16, we met Lydia, a female leader in the church. Verse 4 of chapter 17 tells us that the women leaders believed in Thessalonica. Also, Vs 12 talks about the women who believed. The Jews caused trouble again. Vs 16: Paul was greatly concerned about Athens because of their idolatry. Paul preached on Mars Hill (Vss 22–31).

Chapter 18: Paul was a tent maker by trade. He met Aquila and Priscilla in Corinth and stayed there a while. They were tent makers also. The Jews opposed Paul, so Paul went to the Gentiles (Vs 6).

What did God tell Paul in a vision (Vss 9, 10)? He stayed there one and one-half years. Aquila and Priscilla traveled to Syria with Paul (Vs 18). Paul left them at Ephesus (Vs 19). Aquila and Priscilla taught Apollos about Jesus. Apollos taught many Jews to become believers (Vss 24–28).

Chapter 19: Paul went to Ephesus and taught the people about the Holy Ghost (Vss 1-–8). Remember Acts 16:6 where the Holy Ghost forbade Paul to go to Asia and preach? See how Asia learned and believed (Vs 10). Vss 11–20: God used witch doctors and demons to accomplish His word. The silversmiths were angry because their business suffered when Paul preached against idolatry (Vss 24–40).

Chapter 20: Paul continued to preach and travel. <u>Warning:</u> Stay awake when you are listening to a long –winded preacher (Vs 9). Then what happened (Vss 10–12)? I notice the pronoun WE a lot in Acts. Acts was written by Luke. I believe he must have traveled extensively with Paul. Paul prepared to go to Rome. He called the people of Ephesus together and told them farewell. What was his goal (Vs 24)? He warned them that wolves (human ones) would try to destroy the church (Vss 28–38).

Chapter 21: Vs 4: The disciples at Tyre told Paul not to go to Jerusalem. Vs 15 says that Paul went to Jerusalem. Some Jews started a riot (Vss 27–40) and tried to kill Paul. We see that Paul was a Jew and that he spoke Greek and Hebrew.

Chapter 22: Paul gave his testimony (Vss 1–21). He was also a Roman citizen (Vs 25).

Chapter 23: Vs 6: Paul was a Pharisee. Vs 11: The Lord told Paul that he needed to go to Rome. Vss 12, 13: Some of the Jews made an oath to kill Paul. A commander, Claudias Lysias, ordered an armed escort of 470 men for Paul and wrote a letter of introduction to Governor Felix (Vss 22–35).

Chapter 24: Paul on trial with Governor Felix (Vss 1–23). Paul was imprisoned for two years.

Chapter 25: Festus took over the rule of Felix (Vss 1–5). Vs 6: He ordered Paul to court. Paul appealed his case to Caesar (Vs 11). King Agrippa arrived at Caesarea and Festus told him about Paul (Vss 13–21). King Agrippa requested to hear Paul (Vs 22).

Chapter 26: Paul knew that King Agrippa was an expert in Jewish law. Paul gave his testimony again. Read Vs 28: King Agrippa almost decided to be a Christian.

Chapter 27: Paul was to sail to Italy, but there were many problems on the sea. A cyclonic windstorm threatened the boat and the travelers. Vss 21–44: Paul told them that the boat would be destroyed but that none of the 276 people on board would lose their lives.

Chapter 28: A poisonous snake bit Paul but he shook it off. The chief of the island (Publius) kept them for three days. Publius's father was sick. Paul prayed over him and he was healed. They remained on the island for three months (Vs 11). Vs 16: Paul arrived in Rome and lived in a rented house (not a jail) (Vs 30). He preached (Vs 31).

LESSON THIRTY-NINE
ROMANS

What is an apostle? One who is chosen. Written by Paul to the saints at Rome while on house arrest (Acts 28:30). Paul was unable to travel to the churches so he wrote letters to them to teach, to correct, and to encourage them. He began this letter of sixteen chapters by greeting them (Vs 7). Vs 8 expressed his thanks to God for their faith. He wanted to see them (Vs 11). Read Vs 16. I pray that we claim this today. Are we ashamed of the Gospel of Christ? How are we to live (Vs 17)? I do not know about the history of the Christian church at Rome, but Acts 2:7-11 tells us that there were people from Rome in Jerusalem on the Day of Pentecost. Paul is not credited with starting the church in Rome, but he did accept the responsibility of praying for and teaching them. Paul teaches that God sees all and knows all, that we cannot hide our sin from Him. Vss 21–32 list sins of the people including the worship of other gods. Vs 26 tells us that God gave up the people to their vile immorality. The Word of God stands today. SIN IS SIN.

Chapter 2: Ouch! Vs 1 says that when we judge someone, we condemn ourselves. Paul preached strongly in this chapter. He did not attempt to paint sin as anything but sin (Vss–1-9). Vs 10: Glory and Honor and Peace to whom? Vs 11: God treats everyone the same. A good question for this chapter is do we practice what we preach?

Chapter 3: Vs 2 answers the question in Vs 1. Yes! There are advantages to being a Jew. I have actually heard the argument of Vss 5–9. More than one preacher/evangelist has commented that their background in drugs and deep sin makes them a better Christian than those people who have never lived that lifestyle. My Bible says that God is not a respecter of persons, that God does not judge you any differently than He judges me (Romans 2:11 and Colossians 3:25). Vs 19 says that all are subject to the judgment of God. Read Vss 23, 24.

Chapter 4: Did Abraham have to perform in order to receive salvation? No. He believed and salvation was free to him just as it is free to all who believe (Vss 1–5). Abraham is seen as the father of the Jewish people. I believe the church in Rome had many Jews and they wanted to argue that circumcision was required for salvation (Vss 9–12). Great news! It is not. They could not/would not accept that salvation is free for everyone, that works are not the way to salvation. Paul teaches about Abraham and his faith which was the basis of his salvation (Vss 16–25).

Chapter 5: Vs 1: After we are justified (saved) by faith, we have peace with God. Why should we be glad for tribulation (Vss 2–6)? Hope! Vs 8 declares the fulfillment of the prophecy of Isaiah Chapter 53. Christ died for us! In my opinion, Paul could have stopped there, but being a highly educated man, he wanted to assure that any argument that ever had occurred or ever may occur would be covered. Remember in the gospels, Jesus showed several times that he loves little children. Part of this was their child-like faith (not childish). They do not require long explanations when the subject is God. Unlike adults who must worry their way through every situation. Paul continued to write that Jesus covers all our sins.

Chapter 6: Paul wrote (Vss 1–7) that we are not to continue to sin. Read Vs 10. In Vss 11–23 Paul continued to write about getting rid of sin. Why? Read Vs 23.

Chapter 7: Paul taught against adultery (Vss 1–3). Is lust the same as coveting (Vs 7)? What is concupiscence (Vs 8)? It is strong lust. Read Vs 15. Paul is stating a struggle between the old Paul, a sinner, and the new Paul who was saved by grace. He wanted us to know that we do struggle, but to look to God to clear the struggle to prevent further sin.

Chapter 8: What a glorious promise in Vs 1! Why (Vs 2)? Read Vs 8. Ouch. Who are sons of God (Vs 14)? We have been adopted (Vs 15). How do we know (Vss 16, 17)? Does being a child of God automatically keep us from pain (Vs 22)? Vss 26, 27: Thank you God for your intercession for us. Vs 28 is a verse we all know. Vs 31: Claim this verse. Know this verse. Where is Christ (Vs 34)? Read Vss 35–39: We are more than conquerors through Christ!

Chapter 9: Paul was burdened for the Jewish people even though the majority of his ministry was to the Gentiles. Remember that he was a Jew. If you have access to The Living Bible, read chapter 9 in it. Why weren't more Jews being saved (Vss 32, 33)?

Chapter 10: How difficult is it to be saved (Vs 9, 10, 11, 13)? How does faith come (Vs 17)?

Chapter 11: Vs 1: Paul once again stated his ancestry. Vss 8–10 are prophecies that the Jewish people did not understand. Vss 16–24 talk about the Gentiles being grafted into the Family of God. Just as we can be grafted in, so can the Jews (the branches which had been broken off). God will not turn them away. Vs 33: Paul was being blessed.

Chapter 12: We know this scripture. It has been preached to us many times. God expects 100% from us. How do we prove the perfect will of God (Vs 2)? We are one. Paul warns us in Vs 3 not to think too highly of ourselves. We all have different gifts (functions) within the body of Christ. Vs 10 tells us to love one another. Paul gives us guidelines for living in harmony as Christ's Church. Who has the right to vengeance (Vs 19)? Vs 21 is a capsule of the chapter.

Chapter 13: Obey those in authority. Follow the Ten Commandments. Vs 14: Refrain from earthly lust.

Chapter 14: Paul told the church in Rome (and us) to accept those who want to join even if their beliefs are not exactly like ours (Vss 1–4). He says not to argue with them but to leave those things to God (Vs 10). Vs 17: Why get caught up in arguing about what to eat or drink when the real topic should be righteousness, peace and joy.

Chapter 15: Vs 1: The strong should help the weak. Vs 7: Receive one another. Vs 22: Paul still wanted to go to Rome. He asked them to pray for him (Vss 30–32).

Chapter 16: Paul asked the church to show hospitality to the believers who had worked with him (Vss 1–16). He warned them to discern those who are working against Christ (Vss 17–20). We still need discernment in this today.

LESSON FORTY
FIRST CORINTHIANS

A letter from Paul and Sosthenes to the church at Corinth.

Chapter 1: He was thankful for them (Vs 4). What was his wish for them (Vs 8)? Paul noted that there was contention among the people (Vs 11). He told them that he wasn't sent to baptize but to preach (Vs 17). Vss 18–30 addressed foolishness versus wisdom. Those who are wise by worldly standards are foolish in God's sight. Another reminder that God sees us differently than the world sees us.

Chapter 2: Spiritual wisdom. Do we measure our faith by this world or by the power of God (Vs 5)? Vs 9: We don't know all that God has for us yet. Who teaches us Godly wisdom (Vs 13)?

Chapter 3: Paul lectured the Corinthian church to grow up—to mature in God's will (Vss 1, 2). Division in the church is carnal (physical, sexual, worldly) (Vs 3). We are to be laborers together with God (Vs 9). Vs 11: Jesus is our foundation. We are God's temple (Vs 17).

Chapter 4: Judgment belongs to God. Read Vs 10: fools/wise, weak/strong, honorable/despised depending on who is judging (the world/God).

Chapter 5: Immorality. Fornication (Vs 1). Vs 2: The people weren't concerned to rid the church of fornication. Vs 9: Do not keep company with fornicators. What does our church do about fornication? Do we take a Godly stand (Vs 13)?

Chapter 6: Vss 1–8: Paul teaches us to settle matters among the church not to take each other to court. Vss 9, 10: Who will not inherit the kingdom of God? Vs 11: Some of the church at Corinth (as well as some of us today) have sinned but are saved by God. Hallelujah! We do not have to remain in sin. Who and what is the purpose of the body (Vs 13)? Vs 18: Flee fornication. Why (Vss 19, 20)? A great price.

Chapter 7: Apparently there was much sexual sin within the Corinthian church body—so prevalent that Paul suggested men and women be totally apart (Vs 1). God ordained marriage. He did not mean for everyone to be alone (Vss 2–7). Vs 9: Marriage is better than lusting. Vss 12–17: Paul is giving his opinion. He states in Vs 12 that this is His opinion, not necessarily God's law.

Chapter 8: One of the arguments (contentions) in the Corinthian church was about eating food which was offered to idols. We know that idols are not alive and cannot eat. Vs 8: God doesn't recommend this but neither does he condemn it. This problem: If we eat it, this may be a stumbling block to others, so best to refuse it rather than offend someone.

Chapter 9: Paul talked to the Corinthian church about financial support. He gave lessons that are easy to understand (Vss 7–10). Vs 16: Paul preached whether he was paid or not. He couldn't stop himself. He was so full of the message of Christ that it just rolled out of him (Vss 15, 16). What was his pay (Vs 18)?

Chapter 10: Paul gave a quick review of the Children of Israel in the wilderness and about how God provided for them (Vss 1–7). Vss 8–10: He continued to point out the sins of the Children of Israel and the results of those sins. Do you ever feel that your burden is too heavy? That you are fighting alone, that there is no escape? Read Vs 13. Read it again until you believe it down deep in your soul. Vss 16–18: Paul talks about communion. Then in Vss 19–21 he talks about sacrifices to demons and warns the people to refrain from such. Vs 23: There are things that are legal, but not expedient (good for us/others) or edifying – helpful to build the body of Christ. Think about some things that legally we can do under our current laws but are not in the best interest of anyone (alcohol, narcotics, marijuana, abortion). Vss 31, 32: Whatever we eat or drink, do it to the glory of God.

Chapter 11: A discourse on head coverings. Paul was adamant that a woman should have her head covered (Vss 1–16). Does a woman's hair qualify? Vss 17–34: Paul talks about communion etiquette. There were arguments about this to the point that the church body was harmed. It appears that folks were eating without thought of sharing with the other people. Also, they were drinking the wine to excess—even to the point of drunkenness (vs 21). Communion is not a potluck all-you-can-eat buffet. It is a memorial to Christ and His death on the cross. What is the cost of this gorging and imbibing (Vss 28–31)? Paul's advice (Vss 33, 34).

Chapter 12: Unity and Diversity. We all have been given spiritual gifts. Who can receive a manifestation of the Spirit (Vs 7)? Vss 8–10: A listing of spiritual gifts. Vss 11, 12 says that even though the gifts are different, they are meant to be used together. Vss 13–27: Paul explains this concept using the human body for the object lesson. Then Vs 17 carries that further by stating that we are the body of Christ. Vss 28–31: Working together to edify Christ.

Chapter 13: Everyone is familiar with this chapter. Love is the greatest gift.

Chapter 14: Paul taught concerning unknown languages. He explained that everything we do and say should glorify God and edify the church. What is important (Vs 12)? Vss 18, 19: Paul revealed that he spoke in tongues but realized that it is more important for people to understand than to edify himself. Tongues used incorrectly create confusion (vs 23). Read the last sentence of Vs 26. Vs 22: God is not the author of confusion. Everything should be done in decency and in order.

Chapter 15: Paul preached Christ's life, death and resurrection. He presented an argument for those who wish to argue about the authenticity of Christ. After Christ defeats all the enemies (especially sin and death), He will turn all power back to God the Father (Vss 24–26). Vs 27: All things are under His feet! Vs 35 asks questions that we still hear today—What will we look like? Paul compared us to a seed planted that changes into a plant after the seed dies (Vss 35–44). The new you will be sinless, powerful, spiritual (Vss 42–44). Vss 50–58: Some will not die. The grave will not have the victory but God will have the victory.

Chapter 16: Paul reminded the believers to regularly give support to the leaders and evangelists (Vss 1–3). He reminded them to accept and support Timothy (Vss 10, 11). Paul closed with a blessing on the church at Corinth (Vss 23, 24).

LESSON FORTY-ONE
SECOND CORINTHIANS

Paul and Timothy wrote this 2nd letter to the church at Corinth.

Chapter 1: It began with a blessing on the people. Vs 4: God is the God of comfort both to us and through us to comfort others. Vss 8–10: Paul told the church about the troubles in Asia. Read Acts 19:23–41. In Vs 11, Paul asked for prayer. Who appointed and anointed Paul to be an apostle (Vs 21? Why didn't Paul go again to Corinth (Vs 23)? This is explained more in the next chapter.

Chapter 2: Paul did not go to Corinth again because of a heaviness, a need to rebuke, because he did not want to make them sorrowful (Vss 1, 2). Vs 4: Paul wrote to them in anguish, not to grieve them but that they would know how much he loved them and wanted them to be right with God. Vss 5–8: He asked the church to forgive a man that was causing grief—to love and nurture him so he would not be lost. Why should we forgive and reach out to anyone who has wronged us (Vss 8–11)?

Chapter 3: The lives they lived (and that we live) are testimony of good teaching (Vss 1–3). Vs 5: Where did the power and success derive? What gives us light (Vs 6)? Where is liberty (Vs 17)? Vs 18: The Holy Spirit changes us to shine more brightly.

Chapter 4: Vss 1, 2: Walking and teaching in the truth. Vs 4: The god of this world blinds people to the truth. In Genesis chapter 1, we read that there was a great darkness but that God commanded light. Second Corinthians Chapter 4 Verse 6 says: "For God, who commanded the light to shine out of darkness, hath shined in our hearts, to give the light of the knowledge of the glory of God in the face of Jesus Christ". Read Vss 8–10. Vss 16–18: Even when we are tired, weary, or weak, we are renewed daily. Our troubles are only momentary. Our hope is eternal.

Chapter 5: Vss 1–4: When our earthly bodies are gone, we will have heavenly bodies. How do we walk (Vs 7)? Vs 10: Everyone will appear before the judgment seat. Read Vs 17 until it makes you shout for joy! Vss 18–21: We are reconciled to God.

Chapter 6: When is the day of salvation (Vs 2)? In what incidences should we be approved of God (Vss 4–10)? Vss 14–18: A warning about being unequally yoked.

Chapter 7: Paul urged them and us to cleanse ourselves to perfect holiness (Vs 1). Vss 4–10: Paul was encouraged by the church at Corinth because Titus gave a good report of their desire to follow God. Vs 11: The people were clear with God. Vs 16: Paul rejoiced over the Corinthian church.

Chapter 8: Vss 1–6: Paul told the Corinthians about God's grace to the church in Macedonia. The church at Macedonia was blessing others and Paul encouraged the Corinthian church to do likewise (Vss 6–16). Vss 16–24: Paul sent Titus and two other teachers to Corinth.

Chapter 9: Paul taught about giving because you want to give (Vss 1–5). Vss 6–8: God loves cheerful givers and he provides. Read Vs 15 and repeat it loudly.

Chapter 10: Vs 4: Still true today. We can be mighty through God and destroy the strongholds of Satan. We must cleanse and prepare our minds and hearts for this.

Chapter 11: Vs 1: Paul told them that he had a godly jealousy about them. Vss 4–15: He prayed for them and warned them of false teachers who say that they are of Christ, just like Satan trying to pass himself off as an angel of light. Vss 22–33: Paul gives some of his history. He was a Hebrew, and Israelite, a seed of Abraham. We know from early scriptures that he was also a Jew and a Pharisee. Paul was beaten, stoned, shipwrecked and left in the water for a day and a night. He was robbed, weary, in pain, hungry, thirsty, cold and naked. In addition, he carried the burden of the churches. Still, he carried the news of Christ and stood fast in his faith.

Chapter 12: Vs 7: Paul had a physical affliction, a thorn in the flesh, which he asked God three times to remove. Vs 9: God told him that His grace is sufficient and His strength is perfected in Paul's weakness. Vs 10: Paul accepted this. However, Paul continued to be burdened by the Corinthians for fear they would turn away from God (Vss 20, 21).

Chapter 13: Paul warned them to be diligent, to be perfect, to live peacefully, to do the will of God. Then he blessed them.

LESSON FORTY-TWO

GALATIANS

Written by Paul to the churches in Galatia.

Chapter 1: (Vss 1, 2): All of Paul's letters began by introducing himself and telling us to whom the letter is written. All of them began with a blessing of grace and peace and ended with a blessing of Grace. Vs 4: Why did Jesus give Himself for our sins? Vss 6–9: Some false prophets had come. Vss 11, 12: Where did Paul get his teaching? Vs 24: What happened when Paul preached?

Chapter 2: Is circumcision required to be a Christian (Vs 3)? Vss 4, 5 talk about the fault finders who wanted to confuse the people by teaching that the old Jewish laws had to be followed. Vss 11–14: Did Paul correct Peter? Peter ate with the Gentiles for awhile and then wouldn't eat with them because he was afraid of what the Jews might do. Vs 16: How are we justified? Vs 21: Would we need Christ if just keeping the Jewish laws was sufficient?

Chapter 3: Vs 1: Paul scolded the Galatians for allowing someone (a false prophet) to take their eyes off Jesus. Vs 8: A reminder of God's covenant with Abraham. It says all nations would be blessed—not just Israel. Read that again. It says ALL nations! Who redeemed us from the curse of the law (Vs 13)? Read the promise in Vs 26. Vss 28, 29: We are all one in Christ.

Chapter 4: As heirs, we are sons. We are not just servants. Vss 8–11: Paul asked why they would want to return to following the law after receiving grace? Vss 17–23: Paul was hurt because the people were not firmly grounded in the faith.

Chapter 5: Vs 1: Paul preaches to be free—not under bondage of the law. Vs 4: If you return to living under the law, you have lost the grace of God. Ever hear the saying that one rotten apple will spoil the whole barrel? Read Vs 9. Vs 14: What is the fulfillment of the law? Vs 15: What happens when we backbite? Vs 18: Be led by the Spirit, not the law. Vss 19–21: Works of the flesh are listed. Vss 22, 23: Fruits of the Spirit are listed. Vs 26: Paul warned us about pride.

Chapter 6: Vs 1: How do we restore a person overtaken in a fault? Vss 7,8: We reap what we sew. Vs 10: Paul advises us to do good to everyone. Vss 16–18: Paul ended the letter with a blessing.

LESSON FORTY-THREE
EPHESIANS

A letter to Paul to the saints at Ephesus.

Chapter 1: Vs 4: When were we chosen? How are we to live? Vs 7: Our redemption is through Christ's blood—not the blood of goats or rams or pigeons. Vs 10: When the time comes, all the believers will be gathered together with Christ. What is our purpose (Vs 12)? Vs 15: Paul praised the church at Ephesus for their faith. Vss 16–23: Paul's continual prayer for the Ephesians. He prayed for wisdom for them. He reminded them in Vs 22 that Christ has put everything under His feet.

Chapter 2: Vss 1–3: Who controlled the believers (including us) before being quickened (changed) by God? Vss 4–9: Who do we follow since being quickened? Vs 6: Where do we sit? Vs 8, 9: How (through what) are we saved? Paul reminds the believers at Ephesus (and us) that we were Gentiles, we had no part in the original Covenant, we had no hope, we were without God (Vss 11, 12). How did we become part of God's family (vss 13–22)? We are built upon the cornerstone of Christ to be a Holy Temple of the Lord, for an habitation of God through Christ (Vss 20–22).

Chapter 3: Vss 4–7: Why did Paul write to the saints? Read Vs 9. Read Genesis Chapter 1. Read John Chapter 1. Read first John Chapter 1. Christ has always been. He was with God in the beginning. Vs 11: How long is God's purpose? Vss 13–21: Paul prayed again for the Ephesians (and us). He prayed that they (we) would have spiritual power, that Christ would dwell in our hearts, that we can comprehend this love, and for blessings even greater than we can imagine!

Chapter 4: Vss 1–3: Paul's prayer continued that we be worthy, meek, long-suffering, loving, unified and at peace with each other. Paul taught about being one. Vss 11–13 tell us about the gifts (talents, abilities) that God has given us to work together. Why (Vss 12–16)? Vs 22: Get rid of the old ways. Vs 23: Renew our minds. Vs 24: Become new. Vss 25–32: Paul tells us how to live.

Chapter 5: Vs 2: Walk in love. Vss 3-7: Habits (sins) that cannot be in a believer. Vs 9: What is the fruit of the spirit? Read Vs 5 again. Does this say that being covetous is idolatry? Woe. Vss 11, 12: Don't participate in or even speak of the sins of others except to expose or reprove them. Vs 18: With what are we to be filled? Vss 19–21: We are commanded to sing spiritual songs, to read scripture, to give thanks, to submit to each other. Vss 22–33: Paul gave marriage counseling.

Chapter 6: Vs 2: What is the first commandment with promise? Vs 4: How are we to raise our children? Vss 5–8: How are servants to live and obey? Vs 9: How are masters to live? Vss 10–18: How are we to live? Vs 12: Still true. Vss 19–22: Paul requested prayers of the saints. Vss 23, 24: Paul concluded this letter with blessings.

LESSON FORTY-FOUR

PHILIPPIANS

Written by Paul and Timothy to the saints at Philippi.

Chapter 1: Vss 3–8: Paul shared how much he loved these folks. Vss 9–14: Paul's prayer for them. Vss 12–14: Paul told them that his suffering and imprisonment are positive things in reaching people and that the people are not to be afraid to speak the Word of God. Vss 20–25: Paul wanted to be bold and not ashamed to be a testimony to God. Vss 26–30: He encouraged them to be faithful, courageous, and united in the gospel.

Chapter 2: Vs 5: Paul prayed that they (and us) will love each other, uplift each other, to have the mind of Christ. Vss 6–11: Paul reminds us of the perfect example of Christ. Vss 14–16: Why are we not to murmur and dispute? Vss 19–23: Paul planned to send Timothy to Philppi. He loved him as a son. Vs 24: Paul earnestly wanted to go to Philippi. Vss 25–30: Paul told them that Epaphroditus had been deathly sick, but God healed him. Paul was sending him to Philippi. He asked them to receive him graciously.

Chapter 3: Vs 2: Paul warned us to watch out for dogs (not the four-legged ones, but wicked people). Vss 3–7: The issue of circumcision continued to arise from various leaders saying that the Gentiles could not be Christians because they were not circumcised. God did not call the Gentiles to become Jews. He called them to be Christians. Paul said that the cutting of the foreskin does not make us Christians, but that we do need to cut away our worldly (fleshly) ties. Paul, being a Jew, was circumcised but he realized this is not mandatory for us for salvation. Remember how Paul had persecuted the Christians prior to his Damascus Road experience in Acts Chapter 9? Paul was so excited to be a Christian and his heart's desire was to see the Gentiles learn of/accept salvation. Paul stated that he is not perfect and does not know all that there is to know about God, but that he was working for that goal (Vss 13, 14). Vs 20: Where is our life goal? (Note: Conversation means life.) Vs 21: We will have a glorious body if we stay true to God!

Chapter 4: What does Vs 4 tell us? Vss 6, 7: How do we have the peace of God? Vs 8: What are we to think about (consider, study)? Vs 11: Paul was content wherever he was and no matter his surroundings. We truly have peace when we can say this honestly. Vs 13 is a great motto for us. Paul stated in Vs 15 that the church at Philippi was the only church who reached out to give financially to the ministry. Vs 19: God supplies all our needs! A blessing at the end.

LESSON FORTY-FIVE
COLOSSIANS

Paul and Timothy wrote this letter to the saints and faithful brethren in Christ at Colosse.

Chapter 1: Vss 3–8: Paul knew that this group had great love. Vss 9–12: He prayed that this would continue and for even more spiritual understanding and that they would continue to increase in their knowledge of God.

Chapter 2: Vss 2, 3: In Christ are all the treasures of wisdom and knowledge. Vss 4, 8: Don't let other teachers fool you. Stand firm. Vs 14: What happened to our sins? Vs 15: Who took Satan's power? Vss 16, 17: Don't let people destroy you. The Old Testament law was only a shadow. Vss 20–23: Why try to follow the bonds of rules that are outdated by Christ?

Chapter 3: Look up! Vss 1–3: Keep your eyes on heavenly things. Vs 14: What will happen when Christ appears? Vs 5: Here is another reference to covetousness being idolatry as Paul lists things which must be destroyed. Vs 6: What do the things in Vs 5 cause? Vss 10–17: How do we replace the things in Vss 5, 8, 9? Vss 17–25: A short lesson in family living.

Chapter 4: Vss 2, 3: Continue in prayer. Vss 7–15: Paul listed some of the teachers. Vs 16: Paul requested that this letter be shared with the church at Laodicea. Vs 18: A blessing.

LESSON FORTY-SIX
FIRST AND SECOND THESSALONIANS

FIRST THESSALONIANS

A letter from Paul, Timothy and Silvanus to the church of the Thessalonians. Paul blessed the church and prayed for them, remembering their faith, love and patience. This church had helped the churches of Laodicea and Achaia.

Chapter 2: Vss 2–6: Paul referred to the shameful way that the missionaries had been treated on a former trip to Philippi. Read Acts Chapter 16. Paul spoke plainly. Vs 13: Paul expressed his thanks that the Thessalonians were so faithful even during persecution (Vss 14–16). Vs 20: The church at Thessalonica encouraged Paul.

Chapter 3: Vss 1–5: Paul sent Timothy to help strengthen the church because they were being persecuted. Yet, the church stood strong and this news blessed and uplifted Paul (Vss 6–13).

Chapter 4: Vss 1–8: Paul urges us to refrain from sexual fornication. Vss 13–18: He encourages us to live closer to God every day. He taught about death and life after death. He taught about the second coming of Christ and the resurrection of the dead, that we will meet Him in the air to remain with Him forever.

Chapter 5: Vss 1–6: Paul continued to teach that we do not know God's timing so we must always BE READY. Vs 9: What has God appointed us to do? Vss 10–27: How to live in preparation. Vs 28: Blessing.

SECOND THESSALONIANS

The second letter from Paul, Timothy and Silvanus to the church of the Thessalonians.

Chapter 1: Paul thanked God that the church was growing in faith and love even in the midst of persecution.

Chapter 2: Vss 1–12: Paul warned them (and us) that Satan (the son of perdition) will cause a great falling away from God before the trumpet sounds and Christ returns to redeem His church. Read Vs 8. The wicked will be revealed. Vs 12: What happens to wicked, delusional people? Vss 13–17: How do we remain true to God?

Chapter 3: Vss 1, 2: Paul requested prayer. Vs 6: What to do about non-believer friends. Woe to the lazy (Vs 10). Connect Vs 15 to Vs 6. Vs 18: A blessing.

LESSON FORTY-SEVEN
FIRST AND SECOND TIMOTHY

FIRST TIMOTHY

Paul wrote two letters (First and Second Timothy) to Timothy, his son in faith.

Chapter 1: Vs 3: Timothy was in Ephesus to teach the church to avoid false teachers. Vss 6–11: These false teachers wanted to be famous by giving their own interpretation of the law of Moses. Vss 9, 10: Paul stated that the law is for sinners. He listed a lot of sins. Vs 13: Why did Paul obtain mercy when he had been a persecutor and a blasphemer? Do we claim Vs 15?

Chapter 2: Vss 1, 2: Paul asked for prayers and intercessions for those in authority. Vss 3, 4: How many people does God want to be saved? Vss 9–15: Per Paul (he does not say that the Lord demands this) women are to be quiet and humble. They are not to teach in the church. My personal comment: Where would we be today if not for godly women teachers and workers?

Chapter 3: A bishop is a preacher in this scripture. Vss 1–7: The attributes of a good preacher. Vss 8–13: The requirements to be a deacon.

Chapter 4: Vss 1–3: Paul talks about Christians leaving the faith. Vss 6–16: Paul was teaching Timothy how to teach the church.

Chapter 5: Vss 1, 2: Paul taught Timothy (and us) to honor the older people and to be pure with everyone. Vss 3–16: Study Paul's instructions about social work. Pay special attention to Vs 8. This is where our society has gone wrong. We encourage and support lazy people. The Bible does not support socialism. Vss 19, 20: How are we to handle problems?

Chapter 6: Vss 1, 2: How servants should live. Vs 7: The Bible tells us that we will not take earthly treasures with us when we leave this world. We often hear Vs 10 misquoted. It is not the money that is the root of all evil. It is the love of money. Vss 11–20: Paul continued to teach Timothy how to lead the Church at Ephesus. He ends with a blessing.

SECOND TIMOTHY

Chapter 1: Vss 2–7: Paul was very proud of Timothy. Vs 12: Paul's testimony.

Chapter 2: Vss 1–4: Paul compared Timothy to a good soldier. Vs 9: Even though Paul was bound in jail, the Word of God is not bound. Vs 15: A verse we should all have deep in our hearts. Vs 19: God knows His people.

Chapter 3: Vss 1–13: Paul addressed the Last Days. Does this sound like current events? Vss 16, 17: What is the origin of scripture? Why do we have scripture?

Chapter 4: Vss 1–5: Paul told Timothy to stick with it. Vss 7, 8 are VERY special to me. This was the scripture that we chose for the celebration of life service for my teenage son who died of cancer. So many positive things have come through his suffering and his faith in God. These continue almost thirty years later! I pray that I will live up to this testimony also. Paul was alone except for Luke (Vs 11). Vs 22: Blessing.

LESSON FORTY-EIGHT
TITUS

A letter from Paul to Titus, his son in faith.

Chapter 1: Vss 1–5: Titus had been sent to Crete to teach and to organize the church there. Vss 5, 6: He was to ordain elders and preachers. Vss 6–9: Paul listed the necessary qualifications for these offices. Vs 10, 11: Why was it important for them to be steadfast in doctrine? Vss 12–16: Sounds like there were some people causing dissension.

Chapter 2: Vs 2: How were the older men to behave? Vss 3–5 How and why were the older women to live? Vss 6–8 advises the young men. Vss 9, 10 teach servants. Vss 12–15 give general instructions.

Chapter 3: Vss 1, 2: Paul continued to teach Titus what to teach. Vs 5: According to what were Paul and the other apostles saved? Vss 10, 11: After someone has been disciplined once or twice, what are we to do? Vs 15: Blessing

LESSON FORTY-NINE
PHILEMON

A letter from Paul and Timothy to Philemon, Apphia, and Archippis.

Vs 7: Philemon brought joy to Paul because of his kindness. Vss 10, 11: Paul requested that Philemon show kindness to Onesimus. Then Paul sent Onesimus to help Philemon.

LESSON FIFTY

Hebrews

Who wrote Hebrews? Sounds/reads like Paul but does not follow his format. However, the last four verses of Hebrews truly sound like Paul This is a teaching epistle.

Chapter 1: Vs 1: God spoke in various ways, at various times, to His people. He still does today. Sometimes He speaks through music, sometime by scripture, sometimes through the beauty of nature, sometimes through a small child. Sometimes He speaks in a still, small voice and sometimes through terrible tragedies. The lesson in this verse: GOD SPEAKS TO US! Vss2, 10: One more reference to Jesus's presence at Creation. Vs 3: A glorious description of Jesus. Where is He now? Vss 3–14 are fulfillment of the Old Testament prophecies of Jesus. Vss 8, 11, 12: Jesus is forever. Vs 14: What is an angel? A ministering spirit—not a god.

Chapter 2: Vs 3: If you do not grasp anything else from these lessons, please grasp and consume this. How shall we escape? There is no escape from this judgment if we ignore God. Vss 6–8: Compare to Psalm 8:5, 6 and First Corinthians 15:25. Vs 5: Even the angels are under subjection to Jesus. Vs 9: Jesus died for everyone. Why? Vs 10: To bring man to salvation. If you needed child-raising advice, would you ask someone who has never had a child/raised a child? If your check engine light comes on, do you take it to the CPA? Likewise in Vss 14–18, Jesus is a perfect example and advisor when we go through suffering. He had a human body and He suffered as none of us have suffered.

Chapter 3: Compare the leadership to Moses to the leadership of Jesus. Hebrews 11:23 tells us that both were full of faith. Both were humble. Both had an overwhelming job. Both met with great resistance. Both had a PERSONAL relationship with God. We are commanded to listen to the voice of God and to follow His leading or we will be like the children of Israel who died in the wilderness. They did not get into Canaan. If we are disobedient, we will not get into Heaven. The children of Israel lost faith and turned to idols many times. How many times to we need to be picked up and turned around? (Vss 5–12). Vs 13: Encourage each other in Christ. Why (Vs 14)? Vs 15: Do we wait for a more convenient time? Vss 16-19: Why didn't the Israelites get into Canaan after forty years of traveling?

Chapter 4: Vss 1, 2: Many of the Israelites did not get into Canaan because of unbelief and the lack of faith. Vs 3: Only believers will enter heaven. Vss 7–11: Now is the time to GET READY. Vss 12–15: There is nothing hidden from God. Vs 16: How are we to come before the throne of God? Boldly. Vs 16: What will we find there? MERCY and GRACE.

Chapter 5: Vss 5, 6: Who chose Jesus to be a High Priest? Could Jesus be our Saviour if He had not been perfect (Vss8–10)? Vss 11–14: The writer of Hebrews says that we should be teaching instead of expecting to be bottle fed. Ouch. Is this true today?

Chapter 6: Step up. Mature. Vss 1, 2: Be workers in God's kingdom instead of repeating the basics. Vss 7, 8: Are we good crop ground or just good for thistles? Vs 12: Are we dull or bored spiritually? Vs 19: What is the strong hope of Salvation?

Chapter 7: Who is Melchisedec? A priest, a king, he blessed Abraham (Vss 1–3). Jesus is our High Priest. He did not come from the tribe of Levi like the Old Testament priests, but from God himself (Vss 12–28). Vss 24–28: What are His credentials?

Chapter 8: Jesus is our Covenant. The Old Testament covenant that God made with Abraham was based on law and therefore not permanent. It required animal sacrifices. Jesus made the ultimate sacrifice and replaced the old covenant.

Chapter 9: Vss 1–5 describe the old tabernacle and the furnishings thereof. These were mostly symbols of God, a ritualistic service. Under the new covenant, Christ's blood replaced the blood of sheep and goats. Vss 6–15: His blood covers our sins. He personally intercedes for each of us. Vs 26: He destroyed the power of sin.

Chapter 10: Under the old covenant law, man could not be perfected. The old law required continuous sacrifices. Vs 9 reiterates that Christ replaced the old covenant. Vss 16, 17 should be compared to Jeremiah 31:33, 34. Vs 19: Now we have direct access to the Father. Vss 22–25 tell us to hold fast, to fellowship together, to love one another, and to encourage each other. Vs 31: Consider this terrible thing and stay true to God. Read and study Vss 37–39. He is coming again, not to stay on earth this time. Live by faith and HOLD ON.

Chapter 11: The faith chapter. Vs 1 defines faith. The rest of the chapter gives us examples of people who lived by faith. Why did Moses refuse to be recognized as royalty (Vss 24–26)? There are many more people through the Bible that had faith, but the writer would need lots of time to relate all of them. Vss 32–40: What were some more revelations of faith?

Chapter 12: Vss 1, 2: Many people are watching us, so give your burdens to God, get rid of everything between you and God, especially sin. Put on your running gear of faith so you can run and win this race. Keep your eyes on Jesus Who is sitting at the right hand of His Father. Vss 5, 6:

If God has corrected you, it means He loves you. Endure it. Appreciate it. Read Revelation 3:19. Vs 11: What does the chastening of God produce? Vs 14: What two things are needed to see the Lord? Vss 18–29: We are not facing the Mt Sinai of Moses's day. Remember that no one and nothing was to touch the mountain or they would die. We are facing Mt Zion, the City of God. The city where the redeemed will dwell. Stay on course during this race, we have a firm, unshakeable foundation in God. Win the race. Read Second Timothy 4: 6–8.

Chapter 13: Instructions for living. Commit the wonderful promise of Vs 5 to your heart. Vs 9: When does Jesus change? We are warned to stay away from false teachers. The only way to know is to have a strong, deep faith in God. Vs 15: How often should we sacrifice praise to God? Why (Vs 16)? Who makes us perfect in His will (Vss 20, 21)? Vss 22–25: Sounds so much like it was written by Paul.

LESSON FIFTY-ONE

JAMES

Written by James the Apostle to the twelve tribes (and us).

Chapter 1: Vss 2–4: Why should we be happy when we are tempted? Because temptations bring faith, faith brings patience, patience makes perfection and entirety. If we keep these things in mind, we will be able to stand against temptations in faith. Vs 5: How do we get wisdom? Vss 6–8: What happens when we waiver? Vss 9–11: What happens to the rich who put their faith in their wealth? Vs 12: Another reward when temptations are endured. Vss 13–16: Does God tempt us? Vs 17: Where does every perfect gift derive? Vss 19, 20: How to respond to wrath. Vss 22–25: What happens if we only hear God's word but do nothing about it? Compare Vs 26 to Psalm 34:13.

Chapter 2: Vss 1–10: Do not be partial or judgmental of folks who are different. Why (Vs 10)? Vs 13: How to obtain mercy. Vss 14–26: Faith and works. One supports the other.

Chapter 3: As I write this study, I am so aware not to impose my beliefs but to only write what God inspires. Matthew 5:18 tells us that not even a jot or a tittle (small mark) is to be removed from the Word of God as long as heaven and earth remain. As teachers, we have a great responsibility to God. If we write or teach anything that is not of God, we are responsible for souls. According to Matthew 23:8 Christ is our teacher. Vss 1-–2 teach us to control our tongue (and our pen) so we do not destroy people and destroy our own soul. Unless we live a totally secluded life where we have no contact with anybody in any way, we are all teachers. Family, neighbors, fellow workers are all watching us. Vss 14–16: Envy, strife and bitterness are evil and come from Satan. Vss 17, 18: Attributes of wisdom from God.

Chapter 4: Vss 1–3: Wars, fighting, and lack come from evil lusts. Vs 4: Adulterers and adulteresses are against God (Vs 5). Vss 7–12: Instructions for righteous living. Vss 13–15: Life is short, tomorrow is not promised. If we know to do good and do not do it, is this sin (Vs 17)? Yes.

Chapter 5: Vss 1–5: Woe to the rich if you are hoarding that wealth for yourselves only. Vss 7, 8: Be patient for the Lord's return. Vs 11: The Lord is merciful. Vss 13–16: Do you believe in healing? I do! Read Hebrews 13:8 again. Jesus never changes.

LESSON FIFTY-TWO
FIRST AND SECOND PETER

FIRST PETER

Written by the Apostle Peter, the Rock, to those who are called by God. What does he mean by lively hope in Vs 3? Vs 5: How are we kept? Vss 6–9: Our faith is tried but will end in praise if we remain faithful. Vss 10, 11: The prophets did not understand the message that God gave them, but the prophecies have been and are being fulfilled. Vs 12: Even the angels don't know or understand everything. Vss 14–16: Be holy. Stay holy. Do not return to sin. Vss 18–21: How are we redeemed? Vs 25: How long does the Word of the Lord last?

Chapter 2: Vss 1, 2: Peter says to get rid of evil and to desire the Word of God so we may grow. Vss 4–8: Peter reiterates that Jesus is our cornerstone—not a stumbling block. Also read Isaiah 28:16, Psalm 118:22, and the words of Jesus in Matthew 25:42. Vs 9: What are we? Chosen. Royal. Holy. Peculiar. Maybe Peter wrote this to the Jews who had been scattered. Vss 11, 12 say to live honestly among the Gentiles. However, remember that all Scripture is the inspiration of God (Second Timothy 3:16,17) so we are to abide by this also. Vss 13–20: We are to honor those in authority and to fear God. Vss 24, 25 are fulfillment of prophecy from Isaiah Chapter 53. We cannot ignore the Old Testament because it makes the New Testament even more precious.

Chapter 3: We know that Peter was married because he had a mother in law healed by Jesus in Luke Chapter 4. Vss 1–7: Marriage counseling. This continues in general instructions in Vss 8–22 for holy living.

Chapter 4: We must be ready to suffer. Did you know that sin loses its power if we suffer for God (Vss 1, 2)? Vss 7–19: The end of the world is coming so GET READY.

Chapter 5: Vss 1–4: Peter teaches the elders. Vss 5–10: Admonishing the younger folks. Read Vs 7!

SECOND PETER

Written by Peter to the believers.

Chapter 1: Vs 4: Great and precious promises. Vss 5–7: Have faith, values, knowledge, temperance, patience and godliness. Vs 10: Peter admonishes us to be sure that we are right with God. Vss 12–21: Peter begins preparing the believers for His death. Where did the prophecies derive (Vs 21)?

Chapter 2: Strong warnings throughout this chapter to beware of false prophets. Vs 4 tells us that angels were cast into hell because of sin. Vs 5 tells us that because of sin in the world, only Noah and his family were spared in the flood. Vs 6 tells us that Lot was the only man spared from sinful Sodom and Gomorrah. Beware. There ARE many false teachers.

Chapter 3: Peter warns the people about the last days. He says there will be scoffers—we have them—that are willfully ignorant of God. Why do you think the Lord has waited (Vs 9)? He wants all to come to repentance. Peter continued to admonish all of us to beware, to remain faithful, to look for the coming of the Lord. Vs 18: Peter tells us to grow in grace and the knowledge of God.

LESSON FIFTY-THREE
FIRST, SECOND AND THIRD JOHN

FIRST JOHN

John the Beloved wrote First, Second, and Third John. This book starts very much like the Gospel of John. John apparently thought this concept of Jesus being forever is important. Why did he write (Vs 4)? His writings in Chapter 1 need no explanation. It is simple and straightforward.

Chapter 2: What other reason did John give for writing to us (Vs 1)? Why is it important to follow God's word (Vss 3–6)? John explains in Vss 12–14 why he writes. Vss 22: Who is antichrist? John tells us to continue to live godly lives.

Chapter 3: This chapter sounds like a song. Vs 1: We are sons of God because He loves us! Vs 2: We shall be like God! John wanted to remind the believers (us) to work righteously, to flee the devil, to love one another. Vs 13: He tells us not to worry if the non-believers hate us. How are we to love (Vs 18)?

Chapter 4: Vs 1 warns us about false teacher. We hear a lot about the antichrist in our current times as if there is only one and as if this is a new concept. We see in Vs 3 that the spirit of antichrist was already in the world during biblical times. Why are we able to overcome (Vs 4)? Where is love (Vss 7-12)? What does perfect love do (Vs 18)?

Chapter 5: What is the victory (Vs 4)? Who can overcome (Vs 5)? Vs 7: The three witnesses—The Father, The Word, The Holy Ghost. Who has life (Vs 12)? Once again, why did John write (Vs 13)? Read the warning in Vs 21.

SECOND JOHN

Who is this elect lady and her children? The Church! The Bride of Christ! John tells us to love our brethren. Are we to wish God-speed to those who preach a doctrine other than Christ (Vss 10, 11)?

THIRD JOHN

John wrote this to encourage Gaius, a faithful teacher. He also thanks Demetrius for a good report.

LESSON FIFTY-FOUR
JUDE

Written by James and his brother Jude to the believers because ungodly men were trying to destroy the believers. They called the false teacher brutes and said WOE to them. Who are they (Vs 16)?

LESSON FIFTY-FIVE
THE REVELATION

Chapter 1: Written by John the Beloved while living on the Isle of Patmos to show us what is to come. Vs 3: Those who read The Revelation and pay attention to this prophecy are just as Luke 11:28 states about those who hear and keep the Word of God. Vs 4: This book was written to the churches in Asia. Vs 5: This inspiration is from Jesus Christ. Vs 7: Look up. He will come in the clouds and every eye shall see Him. Does this mean the eyes of the animals also? What did John experience in Vss 10, 11? Vs 11: The Spirit of the Lord told John to write what he saw and heard and to send it to the churches. Vss 12–16: John described Jesus's appearance. Jesus's voice is described as the sound of many waters (Vs 15). Anyone who has heard an overflowing rushing stream has a sense of the majesty of His voice. Vs 16 states that a sharp, two-edged sword came out of His mouth. Is this the Word of God (Hebrews 4:12)? Christ tells us again in Vs 18 that He is forever. Vs 18: What keys does He have? Vs 20: Christ explains the mystery of the seven stars (angels) and the seven candlesticks (churches). We must be very careful to pray for wisdom when we read and study The Revelation because I am not a prophet and there are many conflicting interpretations expounded by people who are not grounded in the Holy Ghost. I pray for discernment. Therefore, my prayer for you is to seek the Spirit of the Lord when you read and study and that God will reveal the message to you plainly. May God bless you richly as you read and study. Above all: GET READY. BE READY. STAY READY.

Chapter 2: Jesus had messages for each of the churches. Remember the Epistles written by the Apostle Paul to the churches to teach them when he could not physically be with them. These writings enhance those Epistles. Vss 1–7 are written to the Church at Ephesus. The church is praised in Vss 2, 3 but they have one fault. They have moved away from their first love of God. Vs 5 warned them to repent or that candlestick (church) will be removed. Read Vs 7. This is how each of the warnings ends in this chapter. We are to listen and to overcome. Vss 8–11 are written to the Church in Smyrna. They are encouraged to stand strong in the persecution from Satan, even if they end up in prison. What is their reward if they are faithful (Vs 10)? Compare Vs 11 to Vs 7. Vss 12–17 are written to the Church at Pergamos. Christ refers again to the sharp two-edged sword. Hebrews

4:12 tells us that this sword is a discerner of our thoughts and the intents of our hearts. Christ is aware that Satan is persecuting the Church at Pergamos, but that most of them are holding fast to God. However, there are some who believe the doctrine of Balaam about eating and fornication. Christ tells them to repent quickly or He will fight them with a sword. Vss 18–29 are written to the Church at Thyatira. Vs 19: The positive attributes of this Church are listed. Vs 20: What happened? Some had submitted to fornication (such a recurring sin even (maybe especially) today. Fornication will separate us from god. Vs 25: Hold on.

Chapter 3: Vss 1–6 are written to the Church at Sardis. Christ calls this a dead church. Woe. Ouch. Do we have dead churches today? Christ says WAKE UP. Christ warns them (us) to repent immediately or they (we) will be punished. Vs 4 tells us that there were a few who had not turned from God. What is their reward (Vs 5)? Vss 7–13 was written to the Church at Philadelphia. They were not a strong Church but they had not turned away from God. Vs 10 tells us that they had patiently obeyed even through persecution. God promised protection for them from the great tribulation. Vs 11: Christ told them to hang on because He is coming soon. Vs 12: What will be the reward for the ones that hold on? Vss 14–22 were written to the Church at Laodicea. They were neither hot nor cold. What does VS 16 say? Vs 19: Who does God rebuke and chasten? Vs 20: An invitation to open our door (heart) to Christ.

Chapter 4: John had a vision of heaven. Vss 7–11 tells us about the beasts that praise God continually. Review Isaiah 6:3.

Chapter 5: Someone was seated on the throne and had a book in His hand. Vss 6–8 say that a lamb (read Isaiah 53:7) took the book. When He did, the beasts and the elders fell down before Him. Vs 8 says they had golden vials full of odors which were the prayers of the saints. Vss 11, 12: How many are counted praising God? Vs 14: How long did they worship?

Chapter 6: How many seals were in the Book (5:1)? It is not my purpose to interpret this chapter. Pray for guidance and wisdom as you read.

Chapter 7: Vss 1–3: An angel cast orders to the other four angels to wait, to hold destruction, until the servants of God are sealed. Read this again! God will cover/protect His own. I have heard many teachings about the 144,000 and who they are. Vs 4 says these are the Children of the twelve tribes of Israel. This does not include us Gentiles. But don't fret. Stay tuned. Read Vs 9 about the people from everywhere. There are too many to count. What do they say (Vs 10)? Vs 14 says these were people who came through the Great Tribulation.

Chapter 8: Vss 1–5: An angel offered up incense and prayer to God. Now that the Children of Israel were protected and those that came through the Great Tribulation were covered, the angels prepared to sound their trumpets. As they sounded, there was hail, fire mingled with blood, one third of the trees were killed, all the grass burned up, a great mountain on fire fell into the sea, one third of the ships were destroyed, a great star fell from heaven. This star was called Wormwood and many men died because this infected the water. One third of the sun, moon and stars were darkened.

An angel flew through the air crying Woe to the people of the earth. This was from the first four trumpets sounding. There were three angels yet to sound their trumpets (Vs 13).

Chapter 9: Vs 1: When the fifth angel sounded the trumpet, a star fell from the sky with a key to the bottomless pit. The air became dark with locusts and scorpions that would sting (Vs 3). Vs 4: What were they commanded? Not to harm any living thing except the people without the seal of God. They could only torment those people for five months. They could not kill them (Vs 5). Vs 6: This torment was so bad that people would pray to die. Vss 7-11: The description of the locusts. Vs 14-21: The sixth angel sounded the trumpet. 200,000,000 horsemen were released to kill one third of the people. How (Vss 18, 19)? Vs 21: Did anyone repent?

Chapter 10: The seventh angel. This one has not sounded the trumpet yet. John was sent to proclaim all of this. He obeyed Christ (The Revelation chapter 1) and wrote all of this in a book which has been passed down for many generations. We still have access to this today.

Chapters 11–20: Read and study. Pray for wisdom and guidance. I will not be guilty of adding or removing even a small mark from the Word of God. (The Revelation 22: 18, 10). I don't know WHEN Christ is coming back, but I know that He promised and that He will. BE PREPARED.

Chapter 21: Vss 1, 2: A new heaven and a new earth. Vs 4: A wonderful promise to the true believer. Vs 7: Be an overcomer. Vss 10–26: The description of the NEW JERUSALEM. Vs 27: Who will be there?

Chapter 22: Vss 1–5: The River of Life. The Lord is the Light. Vss 12, 13, 16 are words of Jesus. Vs 17: How many invitations do we need? There are three in just this verse. COME! How? Vs 20 says QUICKLY.

GET READY. BE READY. STAY READY.

Printed in the United States
By Bookmasters